Economics and Finance of Lifelong Learning

OECD

ORGANISATION FOR ECONOMIC CO-OPERATION AND DEVELOPMENT

ORGANISATION FOR ECONOMIC CO-OPERATION AND DEVELOPMENT

Pursuant to Article 1 of the Convention signed in Paris on 14th December 1960, and which came into force on 30th September 1961, the Organisation for Economic Co-operation and Development (OECD) shall promote policies designed:

– to achieve the highest sustainable economic growth and employment and a rising standard of living in Member countries, while maintaining financial stability, and thus to contribute to the development of the world economy;

– to contribute to sound economic expansion in Member as well as non-member countries in the process of economic development; and

– to contribute to the expansion of world trade on a multilateral, non-discriminatory basis in accordance with international obligations.

The original Member countries of the OECD are Austria, Belgium, Canada, Denmark, France, Germany, Greece, Iceland, Ireland, Italy, Luxembourg, the Netherlands, Norway, Portugal, Spain, Sweden, Switzerland, Turkey, the United Kingdom and the United States. The following countries became Members subsequently through accession at the dates indicated hereafter: Japan (28th April 1964), Finland (28th January 1969), Australia (7th June 1971), New Zealand (29th May 1973), Mexico (18th May 1994), the Czech Republic (21st December 1995), Hungary (7th May 1996), Poland (22nd November 1996), Korea (12th December 1996) and the Slovak Republic (14th December 2000). The Commission of the European Communities takes part in the work of the OECD (Article 13 of the OECD Convention).

Publié en français sous le titre :

L'APPRENTISSAGE TOUT AU LONG DE LA VIE : ASPECTS ÉCONOMIQUES ET FINANCIERS

Foreword

In December 2000, the OECD and Human Resources Development Canada organised in Ottawa an International Conference on "Lifelong Learning as an Affordable Investment", in order to provide a forum in which public policy-makers, employers, and trade unions could debate three broad questions related to society's investment in lifelong learning:

- What resources are likely to be required in order to make lifelong learning for all a reality?
- Under what conditions can that goal be made more affordable to society?
- What is the role of public policy in helping to meet those conditions?

This report addresses these same issues. It examines the economic and financial issues that arise in implementing lifelong learning, and considers how the public and private sectors are actually addressing or might address them. An earlier version was prepared to provide a basis for the debate in the conference. It drew on analyses, findings, and lessons from different components of the Organisation's work on financing lifelong learning, as well as relevant material from the Organisation's thematic reviews on early childhood education and care, transitions from education to work, tertiary education, and adult learning. After the conference, it was revised to incorporate information concerning recent initiatives and policies. The report also includes a summary of the proceedings of the conference as an annex to this volume.

Chapter 1 lays out the broad questions that the report is intended to address. Chapter 2 analyses the important economic and social factors behind the drive for lifelong learning, identifying some current gaps and imbalances that these trends have caused. The following chapter begins to establish a framework for a funding strategy, asking where the funds should come from, discussing some methodological questions related to the size of the tasks to be achieved and discussing some theoretical and practical issues relating to the rationale for government intervention. Chapter 4 examines the costs and benefits of learning at different stages of the life cycle, suggesting reforms and identifying ways in which costs may be reduced and benefits increased in the future, thereby strengthening incentives to invest in lifelong learning. Chapter 5 highlights general funding issues relevant to lifelong learning and examines possible new funding mechanisms. The final chapter examines ways in which policy thinking will have to change to meet the lifelong learning challenge.

This report was prepared by Dr. Donald Verry of the Department of Economics, University College London, United Kingdom, in consultation with Gregory Wurzburg and Abrar Hasan of the OECD Secretariat. The report benefits from the input of OECD Member countries into the Organisation's activity on Alternative Approaches to Financing Lifelong Learning, and from the efforts of the Canadian authorities who co-hosted, with the OECD, the International Conference on "Lifelong Learning as an Affordable Investment".

This report is published on the responsibility of the Secretary-General of the OECD.

Table of Contents

List of Boxes

List of Tables

List of Figures

Chapter 1

Strategies to Make Lifelong Learning an Affordable Investment

1. Introduction

Lifelong learning is a necessity for individuals to ensure their integration into the economic, social and cultural mainstream. Lifelong learning *for all* is necessary to ensure economic, social and cultural cohesion.

When they met in 1996, OECD Education Ministers adopted a mandate to make lifelong learning a reality for all. In so doing, they underlined the importance of learning throughout the lifecycle, and the necessity of public strategies to make learning opportunities accessible to all (OECD, 1996a). As Member countries have taken steps to implement this ambitious mandate, they have been confronted with challenging questions about how to best meet the needs of different learners; how to enrich the quantity and diversity of learning opportunities, without sacrificing quality and equity objectives; how to measure and recognise outcomes from non-formal learning; and how to ensure that diverse aspects of public policy do not work at cross purposes to each other, or to the learning goals of individuals.

One of the most complex challenges relates to resources. In contrast to other far-reaching reforms or new initiatives in education, the lifelong learning mandate changes many parameters at once. It implies quantitative expansion of learning opportunities; qualitative changes in the content of existing educational activities; qualitatively and quantitatively different learning activities and new settings; and changes in the timing of learning activities in the lifecycle of individuals. These developments imply, in turn, a strong likelihood of changes in the costs of providing and participating in education, training and learning activities, and increases in the total outlays by society for such activities. Constraints on and competition for public resources combined with the presence of substantial private returns to certain aspects of lifelong learning imply a need to increase the private share of the overall finance burden.

These and other issues were the subject of an international conference held in Ottawa, Canada in December 2000 on the theme "Lifelong Learning as an Affordable Investment". The conference was co-hosted by the OECD and Human

Resources Development Canada. A summary of proceedings appears as an annex to this report, an earlier version of which served as a background paper for the conference. The broad aim of the current version, which incorporates some conference feedback, remains to address the resource issues that arise as Member countries implement lifelong learning for all.

2. Taking a strategic approach to resource issues

To implement strategies for lifelong learning, policy-makers and social partners need to agree on what they mean by "lifelong learning", and then, ultimately, address three resource questions:

- What resources are likely to be required in order to make lifelong learning for all a reality?
- Under what conditions can the mandate be made affordable to society?
- What is the role of public policy in helping to meet those conditions?

Yet the policy- and decision-making processes and the analyses underlying them are neither neat nor straightforward. Resource issues cannot be approached in isolation from one another as they are highly interdependent. Inevitably, a society's vision of lifelong learning is conditioned by its costs and who bears them, factors that are themselves influenced by policy and institutional arrangements.

This paper raises a series of discrete questions, and addresses them in the context of different "sectors" in which lifelong learning occurs. Each of these questions is outlined below:

- *How does lifelong learning affect past assumptions and practices regarding who pays for learning?* Pre-school education and care is publicly financed in part or in whole in some countries. Publicly financed initial education is universally available at least through upper secondary education; at the tertiary level, it is publicly financed in part or whole, depending on the country. Labour market training for the unemployed is publicly financed. Lifelong learning may shift the usual balance between public and private funding of learning. Pre-school education and care should ideally be universally available in order to ensure that children begin school ready to learn. How might this affect the public vs. private responsibilities for financing? In a lifelong learning perspective, initial education can be seen as something that should be accessible at anytime over an individual's life. Can there be publicly financed entitlements to such learning, regardless of age? Lifelong learning occurs in a greater variety of settings than formal education, many of them non-public. What does this imply for who pays? As learning becomes more common for adults, what criteria should be applied in deciding who pays?

- *How does lifelong learning increase the opportunity for enhancing cost-effectiveness of provision of learning, and increasing its benefits?* Lifelong learning implies an increase in the total volume of learning and, at least in the medium term, the financial resources devoted to it. Successful implementation of lifelong learning strategies depends on strengthening the incentives for public and private investment in learning, *i.e.*, increasing benefits relative to costs. So far, strategies for lifelong learning, often in tandem with other measures (to improve quality of education outcomes, for example), have had positive effects in this regard. Thus, attempts to integrate vocational training and academic studies can improve the quality of upper secondary qualifications, and rationalisation of teaching personnel may reduce unit costs. What are the most important factors that drive economic and non-economic costs and benefits of lifelong learning in various sectors? What approaches show promise for reducing costs (*e.g.* relaxing barriers to entry of new learning providers, use of ICT), and raising benefits (recognition of informal learning, stronger link between lifelong learning outcomes and wage setting in collective bargaining)?

- *What mechanisms facilitate financing of lifelong learning, either out of future benefits or past earnings of employers and individuals, or out of public resources?* Strong incentives to invest in *lifelong* learning are not enough to stimulate such investments if actors do not have access to financial resources. In finding financial resources it is necessary to address the interdependency between investments made at different points in the lifecycle. There are limits to how practical this is, since much of initial education is publicly supported, and much of subsequent learning is privately supported. But there is potential for progress in rationalising the public and private shares separately. For example, on the public side, consolidation of allocations for different levels of education, and decentralisation of allocation decisions might facilitate re-allocation of resources across different levels of education. On the private side, greater accessibility of loans with income-contingent repayment might make it less risky for young persons as well as adults to borrow capital to finance the costs of tertiary education and further training. For working adults and retired persons who are adverse to financing learning through loans, individual learning accounts might allow them to defer some portion of pre-tax income during high earning years, to pay the costs associated with acquiring new qualifications or pursuing leisure courses during retirement. What is being tried? What are the pros and cons of options being considered?

- *What mechanisms and processes make it easier to address the resource issues that cut across ministries and the public and private sectors?* It is difficult to make coherent decisions about resources for lifelong learning because the factors that

11

directly and indirectly affect the incentives and finance for investment in lifelong learning are found in different ministries, and cut across the public and private sectors. In addition to decisions concerning the allocation of resources across levels of education (referred to above), they include decisions concerning the allocation of resources for labour market training and other "non-education" policies that involve human resource development. They also include factors as diverse as the tax treatment of expenditure on early childhood education and care (ECEC), and on adult training; the stance of competition policy regarding barriers to entry of non-traditional education and training providers; telecommunication infrastructure and fees; capital market disclosure policies regarding human resource development by enterprises; and the treatment in collective bargaining of knowledge and know-how acquired by individuals through lifelong learning. Many of these issues require comprehensive, multidisciplinary approaches to documenting and analysing particular problems, and for communication channels and consultation processes that involve all relevant actors. How are governments and social partners dealing with these difficulties?

3. Structure of the report

Chapter 2 analyses some of the economic and social factors behind the drive for lifelong learning, identifying some current gaps and imbalances that these trends have caused. Chapter 3 begins to establish a framework for a funding strategy, asking where the funds should come from, discussing some methodological questions about the size of the tasks to be achieved and discussing some theoretical and practical issues relating to the rationale for government intervention. Chapter 4 examines what we know about costs and benefits of learning at different stages of the life cycle, suggesting some reforms and highlighting ways in which costs may be reduced and benefits increased in the future. Chapter 5 highlights some general funding issues relevant to lifelong learning and examines some possibilities for identifying new funding mechanisms. Chapter 6, which is more speculative than the preceding chapters, examines some ways in which policy thinking will have to change to meet the lifelong learning challenge.

Chapter 2

Economic and Social Forces Driving the Lifelong Learning Initiative

1. Introduction

Economic and social forces currently confronting all OECD countries have increased economic inequality, perceived job insecurity and, in some cases, poverty and social exclusion. In addition, there have been major sectoral reallocations of labour. For many workers the nature of jobs have changed. Most governments would accept that these developments require some policy response. A lifelong learning strategy is potentially one of the most effective of such responses. Potentially, retraining, upgrading and renewal of skills become even better investments than in the past.

A conjunction of economic and social forces underpins the current impetus to lifelong learning in OECD countries. Whether these circumstances are historically unprecedented is debatable. However, except in the unlikely event of these trends reversing themselves of their own accord, lifelong learning represents probably the most effective way of offsetting some of the more harmful effects of the interrelated forces of technical change, globalisation and sectoral shifts in consumption and production.

The renewed interest in the concept of lifelong learning receives some of its impetus from characteristics of the "new labour market". We identify and discuss some of these characteristics[1] in the sub-sections which follow, and then attempt to evaluate important gaps and shortfalls faced by OECD countries in the light of these developments.

2. Growing inequality

Over the last three decades or so the distribution of wage earnings and employment has become more unequal.[2] In particular the position of less qualified workers has deteriorated markedly. There is a vast literature on these questions (see note 1 for some references) and many alternative ways to document it. This is not the place to summarise this literature. Glyn and Salverda (2000) argue

13

convincingly that employment rates at different levels of the educational distribution, and changes in such rates, provide the best index of the relative positions of skilled and unskilled workers. Table I illustrates the disadvantages of the less educated and the changes in their relative position (for males). The table also shows percentage changes in relative wages as measured by annual percentage changes in the D9/D1 decile ratio.

Table 1.   **Employment and earnings inequality in selected OECD countries**

	Employment rates by educational quartile, 1994					Wage dispersion (D9/D1) % change per year	
	Women		Men				
	Q1	Q4	Q1	Q4	Q4-Q1 % change, 1981-1994	1980s	1990s
Canada	40.8	77.4	64.2	86.3	4.5	1.5	−1.4
Denmark	55.5	85.6	65.7	87.6	8.2	0.1	
Finland	50.9	77.1	54.6	80.3	10.7[1]	0.8	−1.3
France	40.5	72.4	60.5	85.0	6.4	0.3	−0.8
Germany (95)	37.4	70.9	71.1	88.2	9.5[1]	−0.6[2]	0.9[2]
Italy	20.1	63.3	60.6	84.7	13.0[1]	−0.1	1.1
Netherlands	30.1	70.9	66.6	86.9	1.5	1.3	1.6
New Zealand	46.3	75.7	67.5	90.3	15.2	2.1	2.1
Norway	56.2	86.1	72.9	90.9	6.7	−0.4	
Spain	22.9	57.3	63.6	80.8	8.6		
Sweden (96)	63.6	87.0	73.1	87.2	−5.2[1]	0.3	1.3
UK	52.0	79.0	65.1	88.3	13.2	2.2	0.7
US	51.2	79.9	70.1	90.6	1.4	2.1	0.9
Japan			89.6	97.6	2.2[1]	0.9	−0.3

1.   Finland, 1982-1994, Germany, 1980-1995, Italy, 1980-1994, Japan, 1979-1982, Sweden, 1981-1994.
2.   West Germany.
Sources: Glyn and Salverda (2000), Glyn (2000).

There are marked differences in employment rates for the least and best educated quartiles. These differences are greater for women than for men (and more variable across countries), probably reflecting, in the main, the greater proportionate increase in economic activity for educated women. Also noteworthy is the fact that these employment rates and their quartile differences are not very different in the US and Europe; greater wage flexibility in the US did not markedly reduce joblessness among the least qualified, relative to the European experience. In terms of *changes* in employment inequality (for men), experience is mixed. Many countries experienced an increase in inequality of between 6% and 15%, but Sweden, the US,[3] Japan and the Netherlands experienced reduced inequality or only small increases. In terms of earning inequality, the US, UK, Canada and New Zealand experienced large increases in the 1980s. Continental European inequality did not increase nearly as much. In most countries the trend to greater inequality was less strong in the 1990s, with Germany, Italy and Sweden being major exceptions.

While there are other contributory causes, it is now quite widely accepted that the empirical evidence points to shifts in the pattern of labour demand being the main cause of this growing inequality.[4] Demand has shifted away from unskilled and semi-skilled workers towards highly skilled (and rewarded) workers. These demand shifts have outweighed supply shifts in the same directions. In some European countries, where wages are less flexible than the US or UK, these demand shifts generate large increases in unemployment among the unskilled. In turn, demand shifts are commonly explained by skill-biased technical change, whereby output is most efficiently produced using higher ratios of skilled to unskilled labour than previously. Thus, substitution towards skilled labour has taken place within industries rather than reflecting, primarily, the decline of less skill-intensive industries. Much of this technical change is of course related to the pervasiveness of information and communications technology (ICT), largely but not exclusively in the service sector of the economy. The high skills that skill-biased technical progress rewards are not purely the technical skills associated with ICT, because the successful application of ICT in many applications requires organisational change and innovation (in both product and process) within the workplace. As well as technical skills, skill-biased technical places a premium on flexibility, adaptability, problem-solving and managerial skills.

Whatever the ultimate causes of widening differentials, the changes are profound and to reverse them by policy interventions would be immensely costly. By way of example, Heckman (1999) has made a back of the envelope calculation for the US of the investment cost, in 1989 dollars, of restoring 1979 earnings ratios between lower education groups and college graduates without reducing the 1989 earnings of college graduates. To restore real earnings for both male and female workers over the age of 25 that are high school educated or less to their 1979 relativity with college graduate earnings (holding the latter constant at the 1989 level) would require an investment of 1.66 trillion 1989 dollars. The cost would be greater if under-25s and the economically inactive were included. These calculations assume a rate of return to human capital investment of 10%. As these are very optimistic rates for low skilled and for older workers and for individuals on government training programmes, these calculations probably underestimate the cost of reversing the increase in the US skill differential since 1979. In terms of numbers of persons, Heckman calculates that, for a 1990 workforce, about 5.4 million persons would have to be transformed to college graduates just to reverse the trend of the previous decade. Thereafter, to maintain the gain in relative wages, about 1 million additional skilled persons need to be added to the workforce each year. Both these factors together (the one-off change phased in and the annual increase to offset the trend against unskilled labour) would have required a total annual increase of skilled persons of 70-80% throughout the 1990s. This is a huge increase. It would require enormous and unaffordable increases in the subsidisation of tertiary educated workers.

Growing wage dispersion makes the focus on lifelong learning particularly relevant. Without counter measures being taken, there is a real possibility of growing polarisation: one group embraces the new technologies and survives and prospers in the "new economy" while another group (in which the elderly, ethnic minorities, and those from disadvantaged socio-economic backgrounds are likely to figure prominently) fails to keep up and is increasingly marginalised. It is highly likely that human capital investments can go some way to preventing such social exclusion. Hobcroft (2000) shows that, in the UK, educational qualifications show a clear and strong relationship to a wide range of indices of adult disadvantage (unemployment experience, being in receipt of welfare benefits, poor housing, early parenthood, etc.) at ages 23 and 33 for both men and women.[5]

3. The growth of service sector employment

The trend away from the production of goods to the production of services has been pervasive and well documented (see OECD, 2000b and references therein). On average, service sector employment now accounts for 65% of employment in OECD countries, approaching three quarters in several. Furthermore, services account for almost all net employment *growth*. However, the consequences of these trends are less easy to categorise, in large part because the service sector itself is so heterogeneous. While there is some convergence across countries in the overall service share, the same cannot be said for service sub-sector shares. Across, and even within, service sub-sectors the quality of jobs and their skill and education requirements vary considerably. Overall, it is true that service sector jobs are predominantly white collar (78% compared to under 30% in the goods producing sectors). As Table 2 shows, skill and educational levels are also considerably higher although there is substantial variability across and within the main sub-sectors of both services and goods production. The ratio of low-skilled workers is much higher in goods production than services, but is also high in personal services. The proportion of university educated workers is substantially higher in services, but this is mainly attributable to the producer services and social service sub-sectors; distributive and personal services have roughly the same proportion of university educated labour as does the goods-producing sector.

Rapid growth in producer services, in particular business services which use new technologies and have high proportions of skilled workers, suggests that if this sub-sector is to continue to be an engine of employment growth it will be essential to avoid skill bottlenecks, for ICT specialists in particular. Clearly, the shift of employment towards services increases the premium on higher levels of formal education. The shift to services is not, overall, a shift towards "bad" jobs. Although the employment trends are not exogenous, and may themselves partly reflect growing levels of human capital, it is probably safe to assert that improved education and training will be necessary to minimise mismatch between the evolving job structure and the qualifications of the workforce.

Table 2.   **OECD averages of skill and educational characteristics, by sector, 1998**

	Total goods-producing sector	Total service sector	Service sub-sectors			
			Producer services	Distributive services	Personal services	Social services
Ratio of low-skill to medium/high skill	1.25	0.45	0.24	0.67	1.00	0.26
Ratio of university to non-university workers	0.07	0.24	0.45	0.09	0.08	0.46

Notes: "Low skill" is ISCED 0-2 and medium/high skill is ISCED 3-7.
       "University" is ISCED 6-7 and non-university ISCED 0-5.
Source: OECD (2000b).

4.   Reorganisation of work within firms

Over the last decade or so, firms in most OECD countries have been engaged in a process of redesigning jobs and restructuring the delegation of responsibility; in short, there have been fundamental changes in the organisation of work. The reorganisation of work can be described in many ways, but the following components (which overlap to some extent) are central:

- A re-orientation from mass production to flexible working (flexible specialisation).
- Increased use of team work and job rotation.
- Job design involving multi-skilling and multi-tasking.[6]
- The decentralisation of decision-making with "flatter" or less hierarchical organisation.
- Greater employee-participation in decision-making.

These structural changes have their counterparts in the management science literature in the analysis of developments such as the replacement of "Tayloristic" with "holistic" organisation, the adoption of "lean production" or "just-in-time production" methods, and the philosophy of total quality management (TQM).

17

Reorganisation of work gives rise to many interesting questions, not least that of identifying the forces which have driven such changes.[7] Understanding these forces is likely to suggest some implications for lifelong learning. Technical change is one of the main driving forces. By providing better information about what other workers in the firm are doing, by establishing communications networks and by providing up-to-date information on customer requirements, the rapid spread of new information and communication technologies has transformed many work-places. Teamworking, multi-tasking and decentralisation of decision-making are all facilitated by these technologies, as is just-in-time manufacturing (via computerised inventory systems). Another purely technical determinant of new work practices is the spread of flexible and programmable tools and equipment. Not only do such features reduce traditional economies of scale by lowering set-up and retooling costs, but they require more versatile and technically proficient workers to operate the more versatile capital. That such new working practices require upgrading of existing skills and retraining may seem obvious. Some support is provided in OECD (1999a) which demonstrates a clear relation between the incidence and intensity of training and flexible work practices. To cite just one example, a US Bureau of Labor Statistics survey in the mid-1990s found that 98% of establishments using new work practices[8] offered formal training opportunities for their workers while only 80% of establishments adopting none of these practices offered training. Furthermore, the intensity of training was greater in the firms adopting new work practices; workers spent four times as many hours in training as did workers in establishments not adopting these practices.

Skill requirements are changing in most jobs. Some examples are obvious: whereas workers in machine shops used to require dexterity and experience to work manually operated machine tools, today's programmed machine tools require their operators to be computer literate and probably have some programming skills as well. Similarly, the job of auto mechanic today requires skills to use computer-based diagnostic tools that are standard in most garages. Office workers today must be familiar with word-processing packages, accounting and billing software and advanced phone systems with conferencing facilities, voice mail, etc. But even in occupations where old technology has survived longer than expected, there are few workers who will not need supplementary skills to function effectively. For example, while in some (but not all) teaching environments the old "chalk and talk" technology has proved remarkably resilient, teachers still need to be computer-literate to access library materials, to keep effective records, to communicate with colleagues and to perform many other aspects of their jobs.

In OECD countries which forecast labour force growth by occupation it is generally found that the occupational groups requiring the most education (associate degree or higher) are the fastest growing. Even so, it will still be true in the foreseeable future that the majority of jobs will require less than degree

18

level education. However, the "basic skills" required in such jobs are changing rapidly; the US Department of Commerce (quoted in US Department of Labor, 1999) has estimated that by 2006, nearly half of all US workers will be employed in industries that produce or intensively use information technology products and services.

Of course the relationship between these technical changes and human capital is a complex one. Not only does new technology require new and more versatile skills, but the trend to ever greater stocks of human capital embodied in the workforce has enabled the successful application and adoption of these technical changes.

In summary, the current rapid rate of technical change has raised the skill requirements of most jobs. Not only has the demand for high tech jobs increased, but the rapid rate of change has placed a premium on flexibility. Most of the jobs created in the first wave of computerisation less than half a century ago no longer exist. Even where traditional skills are still in demand there are few workers who do not require supplementary skills to remain competitive in their current jobs. New approaches to the organisation of work place a premium on flexibility, adaptability, continuous learning, and the ability to transfer experience and skill development between activities. Clearly, this is a world of work that requires and rewards lifelong learning. The policy challenges are to devise strategies to provide workers with the education and training they need to keep their skills current and ensure they do not get stuck in low skilled and low paying jobs. Central to this strategy must be the creation of incentives to keep individuals learning throughout their working lives.

5.   How serious are OECD skill and learning gaps in the face of these trends?

How well are OECD countries prepared to meet the challenges implied by the trends discussed above? We highlight three types of evidence that suggest even the more affluent countries have some weaknesses in the stock of skills and competences that are likely to be required to adapt to new trends that are transforming their economies.

a)   Lack of upper secondary schooling

Firstly we look at the "working age" population (ages 25-64) and ask what proportion has *not* achieved at least upper secondary schooling. Figure I shows this for the whole working age population, while Figure 2 contrasts non-attainment of upper secondary schooling for the whole age group with that in the younger 25-34 age group.

Given that upper secondary education has come to be regarded as virtually indispensable in order to achieve successful labour market outcomes, the figures suggest major shortfalls within the adult populations of many OECD countries.

Figure 1. **Percentage of population aged 25-64 without upper secondary education, 1996**

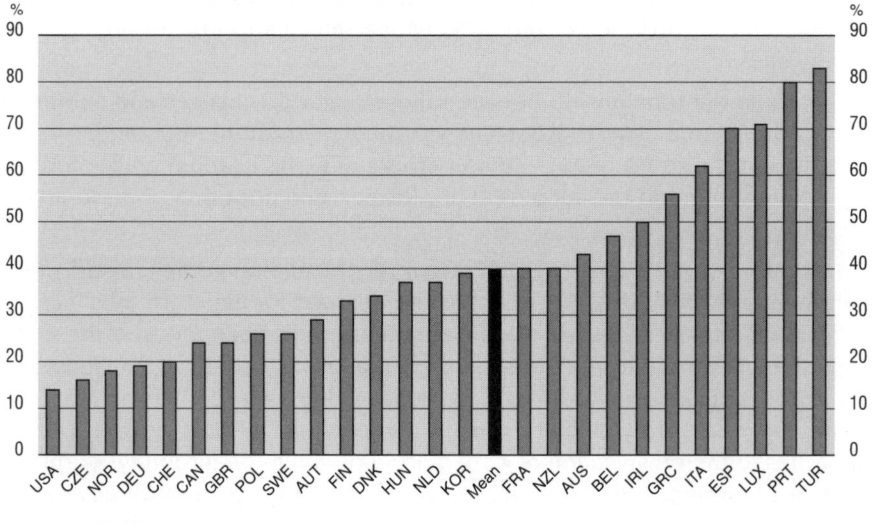

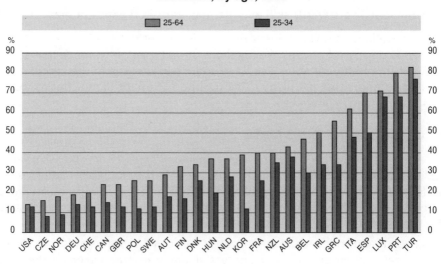

Source: OECD (1998).

Figure 2. **Percentage of population without upper secondary education, by age, 1996**

Source: OECD (1998).

On average 40% of the adult populations of OECD countries are without upper secondary schooling and some relatively affluent OECD countries have higher proportions than this (over 60% in Italy). The second figure shows higher participation for the younger age group; improvements are embodied in younger cohorts. Nevertheless, in half of the countries one quarter or more of the younger age group still is without upper secondary education. Even if we go to a lower age cohort, 20-24 year-olds, the participation rates are only marginally higher than the ones we have shown here for 25-34 year-olds.

b) Failings indicated by international achievement comparisons

Further evidence that our school systems may not be producing satisfactory results comes from international comparisons of student achievement. From as early as the first half of the 1960s such comparisons have shown a wide range of outcomes across OECD countries. Indicators of student performance in mathematics and science have been a particular focus, given the importance of these subjects in today's increasingly technological world. A recent headline-grabbing example came from Alan Greenspan, the US Federal Reserve chairman in testimony, to a congressional committee on education and welfare (*Financial Times*, 21.09.2000). "Substantial progress", he said, "would have to be made to improve primary and secondary education because it's just a matter of time before the bulk of the US economy involved work requiring higher-level, problem solving skills (...). Addressing this issue is crucial for our nation." He backed his arguments by citing data showing US students under-perform on international mathematics and science tests.

Table 3 shows the type of results that have been causing concern. For a fuller discussion of methodology, sources and results see OECD (1997), OECD (2000). See also Prais (1995) for an in-depth discussion of mathematics competence.

The range of achievement is substantial. Pupils in Korea and Japan achieve as highly in the 4th grade as Portuguese students do in the 8th grade. Nor is it the case that countries which rank low in the 4th grade results have the largest increase between the 4th and 8th grades; the second set of scores show Korea and Japan having *extended* their advantage over the other countries. The correlation between the two sets of results reflects, in part, the importance of success in early school years. In terms of ranking, some countries deteriorate between the two ages of testing; the US, for example, has above average results (just) at 4th grade but is well below average (better only than Portugal in our table) by the 8th grade.

As in the case of literacy, these results are likely to reflect a wide range of causal factors. Some of these may be amenable to policy manipulation (teaching methods, curricular emphasis accorded to particular subjects). Other influences are less easy to alter (socio-economic background, students' attitudes, etc.).

21

Table 3.   **Mean mathematics achievement of 4th and 8th grade pupils, 1995**

	4th grade (age 10 approx.)	8th grade (age 14 approx.)	Difference
Korea	471	607	136
Japan	457	605	148
Netherlands	438	541	103
Hungary	410	537	127
Australia	408	530	122
US	407	500	93
Average[1]	398	524	126
Canada	395	527	132
England	376	506	130
Norway	365	503	138
New Zealand	362	508	146
Portugal	340	454	114

1. The mean achievement scores are averaged across a wider range of countries than those shown in the table; 17 countries for the 4th grade and 25 for the 8th grade.
Source: OECD (2000).

c)   *Low skills and skill gaps in the adult population*

In providing an audit of human capital stocks and "educational effort" we have looked at enrolments and qualifications. An alternative indicator, which may highlight some priorities for lifelong learning policy, is to look at what actual skills people have (or lack). There are various ways of doing this. One approach is that followed in a series of studies by the National Institute of Economic and Social Research in the UK (see Prais, 1995). This methodology compares, across selected countries, productivity and workforce qualifications in matched samples of manufacturing plants and service suppliers as well as associated comparisons of training colleges and schools. This approach is useful in highlighting specific weaknesses in teaching and training relative to best practice. The general result of these studies was to emphasise the need to increase the proportions of the workforce with craft and vocational qualifications (rather than prioritise the proportion with university qualifications) and to focus effort on the appropriateness of qualifications and school curricula for those of average ability. Here we concentrate on a related but more general approach to highlighting shortcomings in specific skills and competence – the results of the International Adult Literacy Survey (OECD and Statistics Canada, 1997).

Literacy is broadly defined as "the ability to understand and employ printed information in daily activities at home, at work and in the community". Literacy, so defined, is a means to achieving individual goals and developing individual knowledge and potential. The survey attempts to measure the distributions of three literacy domains:

- *Prose literacy.* The knowledge and skills needed to understand and use information from texts, including editorials, news stories, poems and fiction.

- *Document literacy.* The knowledge and skills required to locate and use information contained in various formats, including job applications, payroll forms, transportation schedules, maps, tables and graphics.

- Quantitative literacy. The knowledge and skills required to apply arithmetic operations, either alone or sequentially to numbers embedded in printed materials, such as balancing a cheque-book, figuring out a tip, completing an order form or determining the amount of interest on a loan from an advertisement.

The IALS testing and scaling method sets a number of tasks within each of these domains, and scales the responses in an interval of 0-500. Each scale was then grouped into five empirically determined literacy levels. We use the lowest two of these (levels I and 2) to represent the incidence of "low level skills" in the adult population. The reader is referred to OECD and Statistics Canada (1997) for full details of these literacy levels, but Table 4 gives descriptions of skills which define the lowest three skill categories and examples of skills which would *not* be generally within the competence of individuals categorised at the lower levels.

Bearing these interpretations of literacy levels in mind, we can look at the distribution of survey results for the OECD countries that participated in the literacy survey. This is done in Figures 3 to 5.

Given the rudimentary nature of the skills embodied in literacy levels I and 2, it is important to note that in all countries in the survey at least a quarter of their adult populations fail to progress beyond these basic skill levels (whichever domain of literacy is chosen). The UK has over 50% of its population at these two basic levels in each domain of literacy. The mean across countries is over 40% in each domain as can be seen in Table 5. Sweden is the only country with less than a tenth of its population in the lowest prose and documentary literacy level; for quantitative literacy Germany joins Sweden. The averages are close to one fifth of the population at the lowest level. Table 5 also shows substantial variation across countries.[9] Many factors could be contributing to these inter-country differences. Both the age distribution and the distribution of education by age differ across countries and, given the association between education and literacy (see below), these differences, *ceteris paribus*, will generate different literacy outcomes.

23

Table 4.   **Definitions and examples of literacy levels in the International Adult Literacy Survey**

	Literacy domain		
	Prose	Document	Quantitative
Level I	Reader required to locate one piece of information in the text, which is identical to or synonymous with the information given in the directive.	Reader required to locate a single piece of information based on a literal match. May be required to enter personal information onto a form.	Reader required to perform a single, relatively simple operation (usually addition) for which the numbers are clearly noted in the given document (or the numbers are provided).
Level 2	Reader required to locate one or more pieces of information in the text but several distractors may be present or low level inferences may be required.	Reader may be required to match a single feature but more distracting information may be present or the match may require low level inference. Again may have to enter information onto a form or cycle through information in a document.	Reader required to perform a single arithmetic operation (usually addition or subtraction) using numbers that are easily located in the text or document.
Level 3	Tasks at this level generally direct the reader to locate information that requires low level inferences or that meets specified conditions. Reader may also be asked to integrate or to compare and contrast information across paragraphs or sections of text.	Some tasks require reader to make literal or synonymous matches but usually reader must take conditional information into account or match on the basis of multiple features of information. May have to integrate information from one or more displays. May have to cycle through document to make multiple responses.	Reader required to perform a single operation. However, the operations more varied than at level 2 (multiplication and division included). Reader may be required to identify two or more numbers from various places in the document.
Example of a task a person at level I could NOT perform:	A level 2 task based on an article about the Impatiens plant asks the reader to identify "what the smooth leaf and stem suggest about the plant". The second para. of the article states "the smooth leaf surfaces and the stems indicate a great need of water". There was some distracting information about other aspects of the plant's appearance.	Reader asked to complete the availability section of a job application form on basis of information provided about the total number of hours they are willing to work, the hours they are available, how they heard about the job and the availability of transport.	Reader is asked to use a weather chart in a newspaper to determine how many degrees warmer today's high temperature is expected to be in Bangkok than in Seoul. (Reader needs to cycle through table and then perform simple substraction.

Table 4. **Definitions and examples of literacy levels in the International Adult Literacy Survey** (*cont.*)

	Literacy domain		
	Prose	Document	Quantitative
Example of a task a person at level 2 could NOT perform:	Given an article about cotton diapers the reader is asked to write down three reasons why the author prefers them to disposable diapers. Inference required as author never explicitly states "I prefer cotton diapers because..."	A Quick Copy requisition form (of a type that might be found in the workplace) is provided and the reader is asked to state whether or not the copy firm would make 300 copies of a document that is 300 pages long. The requisition form states that for documents over 100 pages the maximum number of copies is 200.	Two bar charts are given to the reader, one showing energy production for a group of countries the other showing energy consumption for the same countries. The reader is asked to calculate how much more energy Canada produces than it consumes.

Source: OECD and Statistics Canada (1997).

Of course, both the causes and consequences of low literacy levels are complex, and a detailed analysis is not possible here. In the context of lifelong learning, however, a number of issues arise. There is probably little debate that, in general, low literacy levels can be harmful to individuals' labour market success and quality of life. Indeed the IALS provides clear evidence that literacy is strongly associated with earnings, labour force participation, employment stability, lower unemployment and higher levels of adult education and training. In most cases these effects of literacy on economic outcomes survive in estimates which control for education and background variables such as gender and parental

Table 5. **Means, standard deviations and coefficients of variation for percentage of population at literacy levels 1 and 2, participating countries,[1] 1994-95**

	Prose			Document			Quantitative		
	Level 1	Level 2	1 and 2	Level 1	Level 2	1 and 2	Level 1	Level 2	1 and 2
Mean	19.03	29.44	48.47	19.17	27.42	46.59	17.66	25.95	43.62
Standard deviation	8.26	4.37	11.03	9.80	3.66	11.87	8.63	2.90	10.84
Coefficient of variation	0.43	0.15	0.23	0.51	0.13	0.25	0.49	0.11	0.25

1. For participating countries, see Figures 3 to 5.
Source: OECD and Statistics Canada (1997).

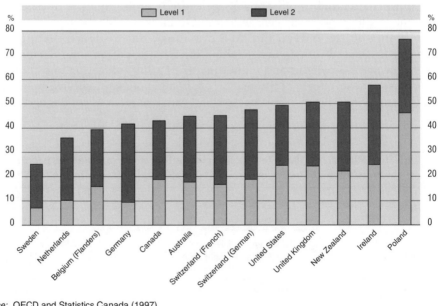

Figure 3. **Percentage of adult population (16-65) at prose literacy levels 1 and 2, 1994-95**

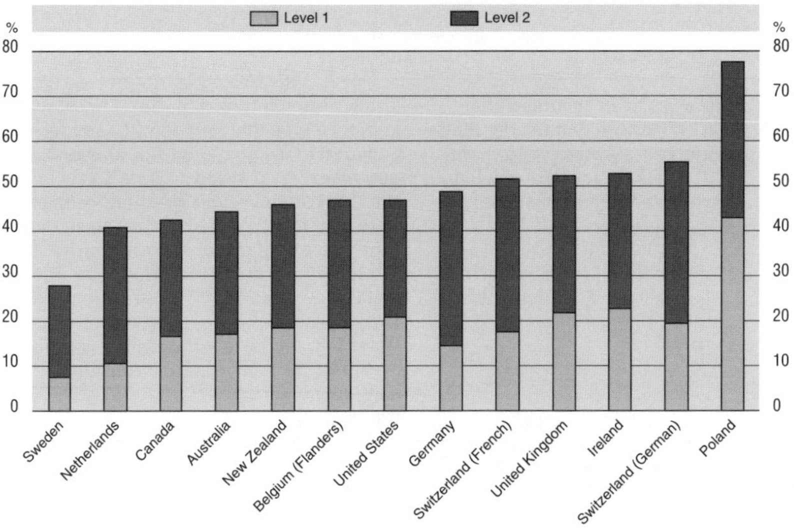

Figure 4. **Percentage of adult population (16-65) at document literacy levels 1 and 2, 1994-95**

Source: OECD and Statistics Canada (1997).

education and occupation. At a broader level it is hard to believe that major skill gaps as evidenced by poor literacy is not a barrier to economic progress and social cohesion. A possible indicator of the latter is provided by IALS results, which suggest, within countries, a positive association between literacy and community participation (as measured by participation in voluntary community activities at least once a month during the year preceding the interview). Looking across countries there appears also to be some association between literacy and community participation.[10] Of course it would be simplistic to suggest that literacy levels are the only or main determinant of community participation; nevertheless the association is suggestive. A positive association between literacy and social cohesion is further suggested by "gradient analysis". In the present context this relates to the relationship between socio-economic background and literacy; gradients are the (standardised) coefficients estimated by regressing literacy on socio-economic indicators such as parental education (itself a proxy for family income and socio-economic status). A stylised picture of the results is shown in the diagram below.

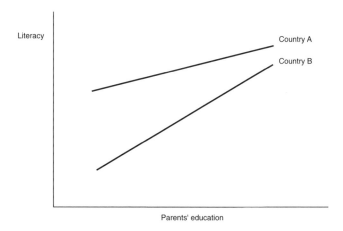

The gradients of the lines are indicators of inequality of literacy outcomes across socio-economic groups (as represented here by parental education). Suppose the lines in the diagram represent young people (say 16-25). Then, in Country B schools and institutions of higher learning are less able to transform the differences that students bring with them; patterns of skills and socio-economic status tend to be reproduced. In Country A the gradient is shallower, indicating that parental education has a smaller impact on literacy outcomes; schools ameliorate

Figure 5. **Percentage of adult population (16-65)**
at quantitative literacy levels 1 and 2, 1994-95

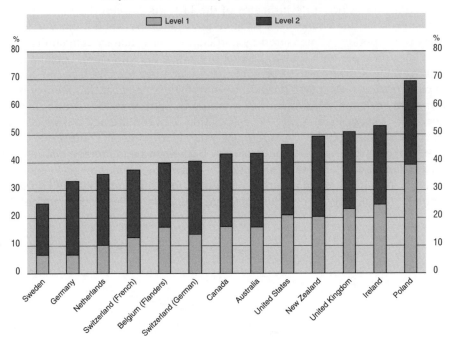

Source: OECD and Statistics Canada (1997).

differences and socio-economic patterns are less likely to be reproduced. The finding of note in the IALS is that countries with high levels of overall literacy tend to
have shallower gradients than countries with lower levels of average literacy. Thus,
in Sweden (an example of an A-type country), youth whose parents had completed
only 8th grade scored, on average, 13% of a standard deviation above the international average document literacy level. In the US (a B-type country), such youths
scored 60% of a standard deviation below the international mean. Note also that
people from advantaged backgrounds (high parental education) tend to do well in
each country. What differentiates countries is the literacy attainment of people from
disadvantaged backgrounds.

One question is whether the skill gaps shown in the tables are simply a reflec-
tion of each country's enrolment ratios at different levels of education. If this were
the case, say if completion of upper secondary school was a virtual guarantee of high
literacy, the policy message would be clear enough – skill gaps could be eliminated

if there were virtually universal completion of upper secondary schooling. This, however, is not the case. Of course there is a broad correlation between formal education and literacy, but there is sufficient variability to suggest enrolment is not a good instrument, on its own, to eliminate skill gaps. In every country in the study there is a wide range of literacy scores *at each level of education*. Table 6 illustrates this; it shows substantial cross-country variation in mean literacy scores by highest level of formal education. The table refers to document literacy, but the results for prose and quantitative literacy are similar. The table shows that while individuals who have not completed upper secondary have, on average, a literacy score which places them about one third into the level 2 range, there is considerable variation across countries. In both Poland and the US (no doubt for different reasons) individuals who have not completed upper secondary will not, on average, attain literacy level 2. On the other hand in Sweden individuals without upper secondary are well into the level 3 range. Thus, those with low levels of education in Poland and the US are at more of a disadvantage than are those with low levels of education in Germany and Sweden. Completing upper secondary will, on average, generate a literacy score that locates them just less than one fifth into the level 2 range. Again, Poland and the US are the exceptions. Completing upper secondary in

Table 6. **Document literacy by education**

	With less than upper secondary		Completed upper secondary
	Mean document score (literacy level)	Percentage who score at level 3 or above	Mean document score (literacy level)
Australia	248.5 (2)	37.6	281.9 (3)
Belgium (Flanders)	250.9 (2)	40.2	288.6 (3)
Canada	227.1 (2)	27.3	288.0 (3)
Germany	276.1 (2)	50.6	295.4 (3)
Ireland	231.5 (2)	23.0	280.5 (3)
Netherlands	262.6 (2)	42.3	302.3 (3)
New Zealand	244.5 (2)	30.3	287.3 (3)
Poland	201.5 (1)	14.0	251.5 (2)
Sweden	280.6 (3)	59.3	308.3 (3)
Switzerland (French)	235.0 (2)	20.6	283.4 (3)
Switzerland (German)	230.6 (2)	24.6	283.2 (3)
United Kingdom	247.4 (2)	36.7	285.5 (3)
United States	199.9 (1)	17.1	266.1 (2)

Note: Skill levels ranges are:
        Level 1: 0-225.
        Level 2: 226-275.
        Level 3: 276-325.
        Level 4: 326-375.
        Level 5: 376-500.
Source: OECD and Statistics Canada (1997), Tables 1.4 and 1.5.

these countries is, on average, not associated with the literacy skills required to achieve level 3.

Conversely, the middle column of figures shows that in each country a sizeable proportion (roughly a third, on average) of individuals who have not completed upper secondary still manage to score high enough on the document literacy test to place them at levels 3, 4 or 5.

On the face of it the fact that on average those completing compulsory schooling only achieve literacy scores placing them in the lower part of the level 2 range does suggest some deficiencies in the schooling regime, although of course non-school factors also contribute. Nevertheless, appropriate responses to poor literacy outcomes would include policies aimed at encouraging students to complete upper secondary schooling, along with curricula reforms aimed at ensuring minimum literacy standards. We expand on this suggestion below.

However, some remedial responses lie elsewhere than with pre-school and formal education, important as these periods are. Consider the effects of age. In most countries, literacy falls from the ages of 40-45. This is partly due to cohort effects – older generations have lower educational attainment and it is possible that their education was also less geared to literacy outcomes. Nevertheless, one result of the IALS is that, *even having standardised for education*, literacy declines with age. This suggests that literacy skills can depreciate over time if not maintained by appropriate practice at home and at work. If skills can decline with age it is not unreasonable to expect that they can be improved by good literacy practices at home and in the workplace. IALS confirms that there is considerable variation across countries, education levels and industries in the extent of literacy engagement at work. Figure 6 shows that even for individuals with a given level of formal education there is considerable variation, both across and within countries, in the extent of literacy practice at work (Box 1).

The rankings we see in this figure are fairly robust, with Germany having high relative levels of literacy engagement at work at all levels of educational attainment. In other countries, such as Sweden and the US, the relationship with formal education is stronger than in Germany; so for persons with tertiary education in these countries the level of literacy engagement at work is roughly the same as for Germany. Literacy engagement at work also varies across industrial sectors, being, on average, particularly high in financial services and low in agriculture. Again there is considerable variability within each sector. Patterns are not uniform across countries. In German manufacturing the median score on the index (relative to the international mean of zero) is 0.3, while in the US it is –0.22. Looking at the differences both within and between countries and sectors the IALS report concludes "Given the role which level of engagement in literacy at work is thought to play in the maintenance and growth of literacy skill in adulthood, the existence of these

Figure 6. **Distribution of index scores for engagement in literacy activities at work for individuals with upper secondary education, 1994-95**

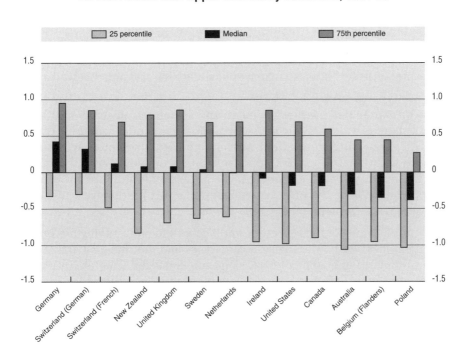

Source: OECD and Statistics Canada (1997).

Box 1.   **The IALS literacy engagement at work index**

IALS respondents aged 16-65 who were working full time were asked a series of questions pertaining to the frequency with which they engaged in specific literacy tasks at work. These included reading magazines or journals, manuals or reference books, diagrams or schematics, reports or articles, reading or writing letters or memos; bills, invoices or budgets; writing reports or articles; estimates or technical specifications; calculating prices, costs or budgets. For each task a scale was constructed to indicate the number of times per week the respondent engaged in the task. The scores were then averaged within each category to provide an "engagement index". For Figure 6 the scores were standardised to have a mean of zero and a standard deviation of 1 at the international level.

31

differences is cause for concern". One can certainly conclude that there is a role for employers, as well as for the formal education system, in developing literacy skills and preventing them from depreciating. The precise details of employer action will need to be researched carefully and tailored to existing literacy levels in each country. However, a comprehensive programme would certainly place a responsibility on employers not only to provide or encourage remedial action for workers with low literacy levels but also take responsibility for ensuring that workers make best use of the literacy skills they do possess.

The IALS provides the most detailed and systematic documentation of skill gaps, but there is widespread corroboration from individual countries. For example, a 1996 American Management Association (AMA) survey of mid and large scale firms found that 19% of job applicants taking employer-administered tests lacked the mathematics and reading skills necessary in the jobs for which they were applying. By 1998 the AMA survey found that this percentage had increased to almost 36% (US Department of Labor, 1999).

The implications of these literacy findings for lifelong learning are profound. We have emphasised how changing technologies and the changing nature of work require continuous upgrading of basic skills and enhanced adaptability. Functionally illiterate workers are highly unlikely to meet these requirements. We are not aware of systematic research showing the payoff for improving literacy, but the large earnings and employment differentials by literacy level documented in the IALS suggest that such investments are likely to be highly profitable, both for individuals and society.

How to tackle the startling shortcomings revealed by the IALS and other surveys is, of course, a complex question. Different approaches are likely to be appropriate in different countries. Are there any general principles? We tentatively suggest the following:

- Early testing to detect young people at risk. We now have quite good knowledge about adult illiteracy, but a forward-looking programme requires early detection so that the problem can be treated before it precipitates a self-reinforcing pattern of low educational, social and economic attainment.

- Prevention is better than cure. This suggests that top priority should be given to raising standards in primary schools. Pupils who leave primary school with inadequate literacy and numeracy will not cope with secondary school curricula nor with the needs of "good" jobs when they enter the labour market. They are likely, on balance, to have poor educational attainment, higher unemployment and lower earnings than their more literate and numerate peers. Reducing illiteracy by the end of primary schooling is partly about raising standards in general. This, in turn, relates to a whole raft of issues from teachers' pay to institutional and management structures.

- *Targeted programmes.* Over and above improving standards across the board, targeted remedial strategies are probably in order. Thus the UK has introduced National Literacy and Numeracy Strategies with specific targets and instruments for dealing with the problem. One aspect which has received considerable attention is the daily Literacy Hour in primary schools. These are structured lessons intended both to reinforce the importance accorded to literacy and to reflect the objectives of the national strategy. The Literacy Hour has a common structure so as to ensure continuity when children change classes or schools. Preliminary results of the National Strategy in primary schools are encouraging.

- *For adults, motivation is crucial.* Illiterate and innumerate adults are often poorly motivated to seek remedial help. National publicity can help to reduce social stigma, information can underline the net benefits in terms of employment, earnings and fuller participation in society and subsidies can improve the private benefit of remedial programmes.

- *Reducing illiteracy will require a range of partners.* Most governments see it as their responsibility to be centrally involved in literacy and numeracy enhancement. Indeed, insofar as the prevention lies in primary and secondary school teaching, the state, *de facto*, has a major responsibility. This probably extends to adult illiteracy as well. Subsidisation of adults on basic skills programmes in further education colleges has been widely agreed to be desirable in the wake of literacy findings, as has utilisation of new technologies to aid in self-diagnosis and subsequent guidance. Unemployment programmes increasingly include literacy screening and skills testing followed by guidance on appropriate courses of action. Like other aspects of lifelong learning, however, partnerships are likely to be more effective than purely state-run and financed initiatives. Employers, trades unions, community organisations, and of course individual families, all have roles to play. Examples range from literacy and skills classes sponsored and hosted by local football clubs to language and culture classes organised by and on behalf of ethnic minorities.

6. Access to information and communication technologies

As the rapid development of information and communication technologies transforms many aspects of life, concern has grown that unequal access to such technologies could lead to a new form of social exclusion. Groups excluded from the Internet will be deprived of access to a whole range of potential benefits, only now becoming apparent. These include access to education, training, financial and health services provided online, the advantages of Internet shopping, cheap communication, entertainment and other leisure services. The possibility of significant

33

proportions of the population being excluded from the benefits of the new technology has led some social commentators to talk of a *digital divide*, with those without access becoming increasingly marginalised.

The current pattern of Internet usage does give some support to the fears of a digital divide. Figure 7 shows a clear correlation between home Internet access and income in the UK.[11] Furthermore, access is growing fastest in the middle of the income distribution (5th to 7th deciles) rather than for the poorest households. Similar, if less pronounced, patterns have been documented in the US. Certain household types also have low usage; in particular one-parent households and retired households (households with two adults and one or more children have the highest levels of Internet access). With many of the lifelong learning initiatives we describe later in the paper dependent in one way or another on familiarity with and access to new ICT, these patterns give cause for some concern.

It is possible that these concerns are premature. The Internet is still a relatively new technology and the normal diffusion pattern is by no means complete; over time one would expect greater usage by income and demographic groups which currently have little or no usage. Furthermore, to the extent that cost is a barrier (the price of PCs is often cited as a deterrent by low income groups),

Figure 7. **Households with home access to the Internet by income decile group, United Kingdom, 1998-99 and 1999-2000**

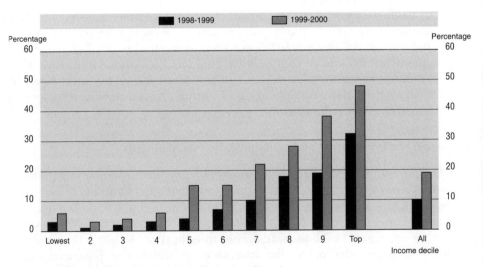

Source: UK Office of National Statistics (Family Expenditure Survey).

emerging technologies which will provide access via digital TV and mobile phones may be expected to relax the financial constraint. The spread of cyber-cafes and free or cheap Internet access in public libraries should have the same effect.

Nevertheless, it should be part of a comprehensive lifelong learning strategy to monitor access to new technologies and to address constraints which could exclude disadvantaged groups from gaining access to lifelong learning initiatives dependent on such technologies.

Notes

1. One development not discussed is the alleged growth in job insecurity and instability. This is partly because many researchers have, in fact, been unable to find hard statistical evidence of such a trend (although perceptions may be important, regardless of the reality). Another reason for not resting a case for augmented lifelong learning on declining job stability is that the phenomenon, to the extent that it exists, is in part cyclical rather than a long-term trend. There is some evidence (Mishel *et al.*, 2001) that the sustained recovery in the US during the 1990s reduced temporary and part-time working and increased longer-tenured jobs. For further evidence on job insecurity see OECD (1997a), Neumark *et al.* (1997), Hipple (1999), Nardone *et al.* (1997) and Nickell (1999).

2. This phenomenon is best documented for the US and UK but there is also evidence (see Gottschalk and Smeeding, 1997) that it is more widespread within the OECD.

3. In the US the employment prospects of the poorly qualified were already poor by the beginning of the 1980s so the small increase in inequality thereafter does not indicate how badly off this group was. Furthermore, during the 1980s their relative earnings fell even though employment rates were relatively stable.

4. See, for example, Berman *et al.* (1998). Nickell and Bell (1995) argue against the demand shift hypothesis, claiming it explains only a modest proportion of the increase in European unemployment. One aspect of their argument is particularly relevant in the lifelong learning context. They note that in the 1980s and first half of the 1990s German men in the bottom of the wage decile earn more than twice as much as American men in a similar position and yet have similar unemployment rates. How can they earn so much and keep their jobs? The answer according to Nickell and Bell is that Germans at the lower end of the ability and education distribution are in fact much better educated than American men (they cite international test scores and literacy levels as evidence). In other words the German system produces a much more compressed distribution of human capital than Britain or the US, enabling the less qualified workers to be employed at higher wages. The superior quality of German vocational education is likely to be a contributing factor.

5. This relation between education and social exclusion is observable even after controlling for a wide range of childhood factors.

6. One consequence of which is that traditional occupational definitions and occupational barriers are breaking down.

7. A somewhat more subtle and technical question is where the rise of multi-tasking leaves the traditional arguments in favour of specialisation. Why have falling costs of communication and co-ordination among workers not resulted in more specialisation? For a theoretical discussion of these issues see Lindbeck and Snower (2000).

8. At least one of the following: worker teams, total quality management, quality circles, peer review of employee performance, worker involvement in purchase decisions, job rotation, just-in-time inventories.

9. The IALS report also documents large variability of literacy scores *within* countries. For many countries the distribution of scores is positively skewed, so that even where the average is relatively high there are many in the population with quite low scores.

10. Sweden, which performs best on literacy scores, has the highest community participation. Poland, which has the lowest literacy scores, also has the lowest extent of community participation.

11. The reason that the lowest income decile actually has slightly higher access than the second decile is probably accounted for by the presence of student households in the former.

Chapter 3

Resource Allocation and Financing Framework: Who Should Pay for Lifelong Learning?

1. Introduction

A serious commitment to lifelong learning will involve doing some new things and doing some old things better. Where are the resources going to come from? One of the themes of this paper is that implementing the lifelong learning vision cannot be the responsibility of governments alone. While governments will continue to make direct contributions to provision and support throughout the education and training spectrum, government resources are finite and some of these will best be used to leverage resources from interested non-government parties. It will act as an enabler and a pump-primer. Both provision and financing will depend on contributions from coalitions of government agencies and a range of social partners.

Public sector resources can come, in principle from one of three sources:

- *"New" resources.* Net increases in the level of real resources devoted to lifelong learning. Where real per capita income is growing, given tax rates and given ratios of spending on education and training to GDP generate real increases in spending. In other words, with unchanged tax and spending rates the so-called "growth dividend" generates net new resources, some of which can be devoted to lifelong learning. Abstracting from growth, financing net increases in lifelong learning spending requires increased taxation or increased borrowing – mechanisms that many governments today are constrained to use sparingly.

- *Reallocation of existing resources between spending categories.* Where the case for expenditure on lifelong learning, or particular components of lifelong learning, can be shown to be sufficiently compelling (because they have high expected social rates of return), it may be justifiable to finance them by transferring resources from other government spending categories.

- *By using existing resources more efficiently.* Economists sometimes refer to this as "X-efficiency" rather than allocational efficiency.

There is surely scope for utilising each of these routes. The mix will vary from country to country, and subsequent sections will attempt to provide some specific examples where each is feasible. The magnitude of the challenge should not be underestimated however. Even the relatively painless route of holding constant tax and spending proportions and allowing growth to generate real spending increases is not an easy one to follow. The 2001 edition of OECD *Education at a Glance* notes that only in a few countries[1] did public expenditure on educational institutions keep up with overall economic growth during the latter half of the 1990s. Furthermore, in the majority of countries increases in educational expenditure have not matched rising numbers of post-high school students; per student expenditure have fallen.

In terms of mobilising private resources, similar general principles apply. Firms, financial institutions and individuals will need to consider whether it is appropriate to devote a larger share of their budgets to lifelong learning expenditure, whether they should substitute lifelong learning expenditure for some of the things they currently do, and whether they could release some funds by doing these existing tasks more efficiently. As stated above, they may be induced to do each of these things by government actions, subsidies, changes in taxation and regulation, etc.

2. Volume and expenditure targets for lifelong learning

To state the obvious, the analysis of funding lifelong learning becomes much clearer if it is known exactly what has to be financed. Unfortunately, generalisation is difficult. Priorities will differ from country to country. Even in a given country there may be many lifelong learning initiatives that governments would like to undertake but no unambiguous menu of what "needs" to be done. Some work conducted in the OECD has attempted to establish minimum benchmarks.[2] This analysis attempts to establish broad orders of magnitude for individual countries about how ambitious their lifelong learning objectives could be and about the extent to which these could be financed from existing resources, rather than having to rely on new sources to mobilise substantial additional resources. This approach is based on estimates of "participation gaps" and "expenditure gaps" that countries would need to close to realise specified lifelong learning scenarios. In essence, the approach has three stages. Firstly, sets of targets for participation in various stages of lifelong learning are formulated for each country. These are framed on OECD median or "good practice" participation rates (the latter typically being defined as "fourth best" in the OECD country rankings). Secondly, these targets are compared with current provision to calculate participation gaps. Thirdly, existing cost data are used to estimate the costs of closing these gaps.

The approach has a number of fairly obvious conceptual and practical difficulties. One of these is that the targets to be fulfilled must be arbitrary, to some extent at least; there is no unambiguous objective in any particular branch of lifelong learning, although for the compulsory schooling there is probably a political consensus that 100% participation is desirable. Where gaps exist, applying historical unit costs may not be a reliable method estimating the expenditure required to close them. This is because *ex post* average costs and *ex ante* marginal costs (the relevant concept) may differ substantially due to economies of scale and other factors (are marginal students more difficult to teach than existing ones?).

For adult education and retraining, setting targets is a very imprecise exercise; appropriate participation will depend on demographics, sectoral employment distribution, the state of the economy, the extent to which firms supply training, and many other factors. Furthermore, even where participation targets can be set, estimating the costs of achieving these is likely to be particularly difficult because of the diverse modes of provision for adults. These vary from government training programmes for the unemployed to informal on-the-job training. Attaching costs to deficit reduction is further complicated by the existence of different cost sharing arrangements in this sector. Reliable estimates of historic unit costs are not generally available, let alone marginal cost estimates. In the event, for adults the approach constructs two indices for the size of the task confronting countries with respect to adult lifelong learning policy. The first of these expresses the deficit in adult lifelong learning in terms of the proportion of adults (ages 25-64) with less than upper secondary education and the proportion with adult literacy below level 3 (see Chapter 2 above). The second approach uses information on lifetime training expectancy (measured in hours) to establish good practice benchmarks. Many of these difficulties in establishing what needs to be done in adult lifelong learning also apply to ECEC where there is little consensus about what constitutes optimal provision and where costing is complicated by heterogeneous modes of provision.

The usefulness of the general approach discussed above is not so much in providing precise costings of different scenarios, but rather in establishing broad orders of magnitude of the scale of the task facing different countries. These are best thought of as reference points or benchmarks; except for the poorest countries with the largest shortfalls in current provision[3] they may be regarded as minimum programmes to achieve acceptable lifelong learning provision. The implied programmes emerging from this exercise contribute to an ongoing policy formulation process. If the implied costings of a given lifelong learning scenario with its implied targets turns out to place prohibitively demands on the public purse, policy-makers will need to scale down their objectives, consider methods for achieving them at lower costs to the public sector, or a combination of the two.

3. Arguments for government intervention in lifelong learning provision

A theme of this paper is that the funding of lifelong learning cannot rest with governments alone. Nevertheless, it is worth considering whether any principles can be established which will spell out certain types of funding where governments need to be involved if certain objectives are to be achieved. In practice, governments intervene in the financing, supply and regulation of education for a number of reasons, including the seeking of political advantage. In purely economic terms there is a case for such intervention when the amount of a given type of lifelong learning resulting from private choices differs from the socially optimal amount. Why might these two amounts differ? The socially optimal amount is determined by equating the rate of return on the investment[4] with the return on the best alternative that has to be foregone by undertaking the investment. Similarly, the privately optimal amount of lifelong learning is determined where the private rate of return to the lifelong learning investment is equal to the private discount rate. The reason these two amounts can differ boils down to "market failure", appropriately defined. Traditionally, market failure is defined in terms of efficiency alone, in which case equity considerations constitute additional grounds for government action. If poverty and unequal earnings are themselves defined as being market failures, then all government intervention can be thought of as being directed at the correction of such failures. In the following two sections we consider in broad terms some of the main efficiency and equity arguments for government intervention in the supply and/or financing of lifelong learning. Some of these arguments are fleshed out in Chapter 4 in relation to specific sectors.

a) Efficiency arguments for government intervention in lifelong learning

When considering possible market failures which could justify government intervention, we usually think of the market for the particular type of human capital on which the analysis focuses; the market for ECEC, for tertiary education, for training, etc. However, imperfections in related markets, capital and labour markets in particular, spill over in to these markets. In the human capital market the demand price can be thought of as the present value of the earnings gain the investment generates, while the supply is the marginal cost to individuals or firms of increasing human capital by some given amount. In the absence of either capital or labour market imperfections investors will augment their human capital up to the point where the price they pay (directly or in terms of foregone earnings) is equal to the present value of the earnings gain associated with the training. Thus, the marginal cost of the investment is equal to the present value of its marginal benefits. This is a first best optimum – where markets work perfectly private and social optima do not diverge. In the real world a variety of market failures prevent the attainment of this happy outcome. What follows is a more or less standard list of such failures[5] that may provide a rationale for government intervention. Subsequently, we will consider in more detail how these relate to particular phases of the life cycle. The point here is that different types of market failure are relevant to different types of education, learning and training; hence the rationale for intervention will differ for different components of lifelong learning.

In considering the following arguments that are often used to justify government intervention, it is important to use the appropriate base-line or starting point. Take the case of educational externalities. The existence of an externality does not, in itself, justify intervention. One has to ask *whether the externality is relevant at the particular margin under consideration.* Thus, while it is no doubt true that there are substantial externalities in having a literate society, these externalities are no longer marginally relevant in most OECD countries where primary and lower secondary education are near-universal (notwithstanding the evidence presented in Chapter 2 showing substantial pockets of adult illiteracy). While such externalities could justify government supply or subsidisation in countries with low enrolment rates in primary education, they are not, in general, relevant to OECD countries. Similar considerations apply to other arguments justifying government intervention; one must always ask whether the arguments apply given the actual starting point. The relevant policy question is very often not "is government intervention justified" but "is *further* government intervention justified, given existing conditions".

Capital market imperfections

If it were the case that the rates at which individuals could borrow to finance a given component of lifelong learning were substantially greater than the social discount rate, then, *ceteris paribus*, individuals left to themselves would under-invest in training. The social discount rate is conveniently thought of as some weighted average of the shadow price of consumption (often in turn approximated by the yield on government bonds) and the borrowing rate faced by corporate borrowers. The borrowing rate faced by individuals wishing to finance lifelong learning is likely to exceed both components of the social discount rate, suggesting the required return to such lifelong learning investments is in turn greater than the social discount rate. High discount rates increase the costs of income smoothing, and some combinations of costs and benefits that would induce investment with perfect capital markets are now rejected. The amount of investments is therefore less than its socially desirable level.

Why is it that individuals who wish to finance human capital investments face high borrowing rates? The classic answer is that, unlike other forms of capital, human capital cannot act as collateral for loans. Except in the irrelevant case of slavery, there is no equivalent to the possibility of securing the loan by repossessing the capital in the case of default, the means by which loans are secured in other markets, the housing market being a prime example. In the case of formal education and early job market training it is difficult for trainees to finance training, directly or indirectly (by accepting low wages), from personal savings, because these investments are made relatively early in the life cycle when personal savings are likely to be low or non-existent.

Borrowing constraints are likely to have a differing impact depending on family income and socio-economic background, introducing equity as well as efficiency considerations. This point is often made with regard to tertiary education, but really the argument applies to many of the lifelong learning investments at different stages in the life cycle. The basic argument is that children from more affluent backgrounds have access to funds that are not available to children from poorer families, making costs of funds higher for these children and as a consequence limiting their access to tertiary education. While it is true that children in more affluent families are dependent on the goodwill of their parents to access such funds, it is true in general that to some degree there is a consumption element in parental spending on children's education. Although there are exceptions, it is generally true that families with higher incomes buy more and better quality education for their children.

There are instances where the effects of borrowing constraints have been overstated. In the US, for example, although that country has high participation in tertiary education by international standards, it is still true that the children of disadvantaged groups are underrepresented. Is this because they face borrowing constraints? In part perhaps, but the existence of generous scholarships and cheap loans for disadvantaged students suggests that one must look elsewhere for the explanation of low participation of certain groups in tertiary education.

Nevertheless, there can be little doubt that borrowing constraints do affect individuals' willingness and ability to make lifelong learning investments. Two specific financing mechanisms we advocate in subsequent sections – income-contingent loans in tertiary education and individual learning accounts to finance investments for individuals in the labour market – can be thought of as specific attempts of governments to counteract the borrowing difficulties faced by individuals wishing to invest in learning.

Risk and uncertainty[6]

The argument in the preceding paragraphs abstracts from risk. Of course, in an objective sense, the returns to lifelong learning investment are uncertain. This uncertainty has at least two major components. Firstly, the demand for skills fluctuates; arguably, the demand is particularly volatile today as many economies are in a state of major sectoral employment reallocation due to the ICT "revolution". Secondly, individuals are uncertain of their abilities to master and profit from their lifelong learning investments. Under such circumstances the utility of expected returns is reduced by risk. As with capital constraints, the amount of lifelong learning demanded by individuals is less than it would be in the absence of such uncertainty.

It is not obvious that such risks are greater for lifelong learning investments than for non-human capital investments. However, even if they are not, individuals are likely to be more risk averse than firms or governments, the former protected by limited liability,[7] the latter able to spread risk more effectively than either individuals or firms. If governments believe that lifelong learning is inhibited by excessive risk-aversion on the part of potential investors, this can be offset either by straight subsidies (the government will get some return in terms of higher tax revenues from augmented average earnings) or by income-contingent loans. The latter effectively reduce or eliminate risk to the investor, depending on the details of the loan scheme.

A related source of under-investment arises where individuals underestimate the returns to making lifelong learning investments or, equivalently, the labour market risks of not training or retraining in a world of rapidly changing labour demand. Again in such circumstances they will under-invest. There is little evidence of any systematic misperceptions of the returns to lifelong learning investments. However, it is not implausible that individuals fail to appreciate the effects of technical change, globalisation and other factors that generate income and employment risks to them.

Other information issues

Informational asymmetries often exist between demanders of particular types of lifelong learning and suppliers. Our analysis so far has recognised that even for a given quantity and quality of lifelong learning investment the benefits are uncertain because of fluctuations in future labour demand and/or in individuals' own knowledge of their abilities. Informational asymmetries, by contrast, are structurally related to the complexity of the service being provided or the intrinsic difficulties of monitoring quality. For example, firms and other training providers know more, *ex ante*, than trainees about the amounts and quality of training that will be received on the job, the suppliers of ECEC know more than parents about the content and quality of services provided (and monitoring is difficult or expensive). Such lack of knowledge is likely to act as a disincentive for individuals to pay for investments directly or by accepting lower wages while investing. Government regulation of lifelong learning suppliers' standards may be called for in such circumstances (Malcolmson *et al.*, 1997).

Asymmetrical information can interact with capital and labour market imperfections to influence outcomes. Take the case of training. Suppose, not unreasonably, that the firm that supplies the training has more accurate knowledge than other firms of the trained worker's productivity. This provides the training firm with some monopsony power and enables it to pay less than the value of marginal product without necessarily losing the trained worker. By reducing the demand for

45

training more than supply[8] increases, this can generate sub-optimal training, but where workers are credit constrained it can lead to an overall increase in training. The intuition here is that capital market constraints have reduced training to some minimal level so that reductions in expected returns have little additional impact. On the other hand supply increases, so the net effect is positive.

Taxation

While taxes reduce both the opportunity cost and the returns for lifelong learning investments made by individuals in the labour force, the returns are likely to be disproportionately reduced,[9] implying private returns less than social returns, the latter being calculated exclusive of taxes. Again, the consequence is under-investment and a possible rationale for government subsidisation. We argue in the final section of this paper that governments need to audit their tax systems to determine how lifelong learning investment is affected at different stages of the life cycle.

Externalities

Where there are gains to society at large over and above those received by individual investors in lifelong learning (and these are not outweighed by the excess of costs to society less the costs to the individual) then individual investments will be less than optimal from a social point of view. Under such circumstances governments may wish to provide incentives for individuals to increase their investments, perhaps by subsidising their costs. Such arguments are freely used by interested parties when arguing that governments should provide greater support to the activities they favour. However, the existence of such externalities is often asserted rather than supported by empirical evidence. For example in the case of tertiary education it is often argued that society gains as a whole from having a highly skilled and trained workforce. Undoubtedly it does, but it does not follow from this that tertiary graduates do not reap these returns in terms of private benefits (earnings gains). It is a *non sequitor* to argue that private investments in tertiary education are insufficient because such education is important in general social and economic terms.

In the lifelong learning context one area where empirical evidence points to the existence of genuine externalities is ECEC, because early learning breeds success in subsequent education and because there is evidence that high quality pre-school programmes produce longer term social gains such as reduced teen pregnancies, reduced incidence of criminal activity, etc. In Chapter 4 we discuss an evaluation of the Perry Preschool Programme in the US which shows the net present value of participating in the programme to taxpayers and crime victims is over four times as large as the present value of net benefits to programme participants. In general,

ECEC would appear to be the component of lifelong learning where arguments for government support on externality grounds are strongest.

Other externality-type arguments apply to other aspects of lifelong learning. A well-known example is the free-riding problem relating to job training. In fact this argument is not as straightforward as is sometimes claimed. Standard economic analysis of training distinguishes between *general training*, whereby a trainee's productivity is increased wherever the trainee is employed subsequently and *specific training*, which only increases productivity in the firm providing the training. In the latter case the firm can pay the trainee less than his or her marginal product post-training because productivity is increased in the training firm only. The floor to the wage is set by productivity in outside firms. Firms can therefore finance such training without fear of losing their trained workers to competitors. There is no reason to presume that there will be insufficient specific training. In the case of general training however, the fact that a trainee's productivity is increased irrespective of where post-training employment occurs reduces or eliminates the incentives for firms to finance such training. Other firms could bid away the trained workers, profiting from their enhanced productivity without having contributed to the costs of training, *i.e.* free-riding on the firms who actually pay for the training. Fearing this, firms will be unwilling to invest in providing general training to their employees. We cite this argument because it has been influential in formulating government training policy. Strictly speaking, however, the poaching argument only applies to *employer* funding of general training. As the trainees benefit from the training – they are paid higher wages in line with their increased productivity – they ought to be prepared to finance it. The obvious way of doing so is by accepting lower wages during the training period. Thus, as in the case of firm-specific training there is no *prima facie* case for believing that there will be insufficient general training if decisions are left to private agents. Hence there is no need for government intervention.[10] In the case where training is purely firm specific or truly general and labour markets are perfectly competitive, the free riding argument for intervention is incorrect.

Nevertheless, the poaching argument has held considerable sway with policymakers. Believing that actual or anticipated poaching inhibits firms' supply of training, many governments[11] reacted by utilising either regulation or a system of levies and grants to compel employers to increase training.

This rationale is more compelling when labour market imperfections generate a genuine externality. Suppose labour markets are imperfectly competitive in the sense that, although firms compete for workers, this competition is insufficient to force the wage up to the value of the workers marginal product.[12] Under these circumstances, the basic Becker argument that firms will not finance general training breaks down and a possible externality arises. When firms are able to pay their workers less than the value of marginal product, even general training can benefit

47

the firm if it increases productivity by more than the accompanying increase in the wage.[13] Firms in such markets would not automatically lose a worker who is paid less than the value of his or her marginal product. On its own this increases the supply of training by firms – they now have an incentive to provide transferable training which they do not when labour markets are perfectly competitive. However, if some generally trained workers choose to leave the firms that trained them, the firms to which they move will share the benefits of training without having incurred any of the costs. The training firm does not count the benefit to the free riders. Thus the argument that free-riding leads to sub-optimal training is resurrected.[14] Levies or subsidies to trainees can, under these circumstances, internalise the externality and increase the amount of training supplied by firms. Because firms are making abnormal profits, any subsidies to firms can be recovered, at least in part, by a tax on profits.

Two other arguments in favour of government intervention in the training market relate to *externalities of market size* and to *unemployment*. The former argument rests on the proposition that a larger pool of skilled workers reduces the expected costs to firms of finding suitably trained workers to fill job slots, independently of the price of skilled labour itself. As individuals and firms do not take this into account when making their training investment decisions, it is quite conceivable that there will be insufficient training from the social point of view. The unemployment argument asserts that where unskilled workers suffer substantial unemployment while skilled workers do not, training an unskilled worker to qualify for a skilled job has greater social than private net benefits. The essential point is that on the cost side the economy loses no output in the unskilled labour market due to the excess of labour supply. Correspondingly, on the benefit side the economy gains the full marginal product of the newly trained worker rather than the productivity *differential* between skilled and unskilled workers, which would be the benefit of such training in a labour market with no unemployment.

Intervention in employment training

When training is sub-optimal due to capital market imperfections, the government can either directly offset capital market imperfections by supplying loans at below market rates to potential trainees or by subsidising training costs. At least some of the cost of this subsidy can be recovered by taxes on post-training wages. Directly offsetting the effects of risk by providing income insurance is less attractive because of moral hazard problems.

A broader view of the role of government in lifelong learning

To complete this section on the role of the state a more speculative note is sounded. Our analysis of the rationale for government intervention has followed the conventional approach of the correction of market failure. It is, however, possible to take a broader view of the role of the state in lifelong learning than simply as an agent to internalise externalities and offset capital market failures. For example, basing their argument on the role of governments in promoting education and training in a sample of Asian "tiger" economies (Korea, Singapore and Taiwan), Green et al. (1999), argue that "given the long-term and social nature of the skill formation process and an economy's needs for the rapid expansion of skills, the state can under certain circumstances perform a matching function for skills supply and demand, superior to that afforded by market processes." One example provided by the authors relates directly to lifelong learning in Singapore in the 1980s. As the economy converged to OECD growth rates and towards frontier technologies, it was perceived that there remained many workers with inadequate basic skills (in mathematics, literacy and IT) who were likely to become vulnerable at lower (but sustainable) growth rates. In response, the Singaporean government's Vocational and Industrial Training Board launched a series of training schemes to upgrade the skills of mature workers still in employment who had not progressed beyond primary education in the 1950s. Financed in part by a levy on the employment of low paid labour, the programmes, both on and off the job, enabled such workers to continue their education to secondary level or to augment their work-related skills. Another example of successful strategic government intervention was the role of the Korean government in promoting vocational education, offsetting the private preferences of pupils and their parents for more academic learning. Academic education is sometimes preferred for reasons of pure status, but vocational education may also be eschewed by individuals as being too risky. In such cases the state may be less risk-averse and may be able to modify private decisions by promoting a comprehensive lifelong learning strategy which partially insures individuals against the risks of uncertain human capital investments.

The conditions which made widespread state intervention in education and training successful in the Asian tiger economies are not likely to apply widely throughout the OECD economies. Indeed, current trends within the Asian economies are towards more decentralised decision-making. Nevertheless, where it can be legitimately argued that the state should take a longer view than private agents and/or that the state possesses some informational advantage or where it can diversify risks to a greater extent, there may be a more general strategic role for the state than is implied by conventional analysis. At a general level, this is likely to require the state not to take as exogenous the preferences of individuals and firms but to promote a culture of lifelong learning on both sides of the labour market. This will require further integration of educational and industrial policy and the creation of partnership institutions such as national skills task forces in which the main interested parties can co-operate in diagnosing current and expected skills bottlenecks and devising lifelong learning solutions.

49

b) *Equity arguments for government intervention in lifelong learning*

We know as a technical matter (albeit under fairly restrictive conditions) that competitive markets deliver an efficient allocation of resources in the sense that resources cannot be reallocated in such a way as to make one individual or group of individuals better off without making another individual or group worse off. While efficiency in this (Pareto) sense is generally desirable it tells us nothing about the fairness of the resulting distribution. Most governments do have equity or fairness objectives as well as pursuing efficiency, although different political parties and different countries will assign different weights to efficiency and equity objectives. Nevertheless, a number of equity issues arise in the lifelong learning context. Such considerations will influence policy. They may for example induce governments to pursue lifelong learning programmes even where the conventionally calculated rates of return are too low to justify proceeding on efficiency grounds.

Equity here is not conceived purely in terms of some summary measure (such as the Gini coefficient) of the distribution of household incomes. There is concern for equality of access to all levels of lifelong learning and ensuring that no group is excluded from the opportunities and benefits that lifelong learning can provide. Groups that risk exclusion, to different extents in different countries, include older persons, those with poor initial education, the long-term unemployed and (to a lesser extent than in the past) women. Many countries already have in place policies that attempt to reduce passive benefit reliance among the vulnerable groups and draw them into training, work experience and eventually stable employment. Due to public sector budget constraints the pursuit of equity objectives is likely to take the form of targeted or means-tested support for lifelong learning costs rather than universal entitlements, in spite of some well-known disadvantages of means testing (low take up, poverty traps, etc.).

Equity and equality of opportunity is probably the rationale for the central role taken by the state in the provision of primary and secondary schooling. We do question below whether equity really requires government *provision* rather than financial support and argue that a greater measure of competitive supply could be introduced into compulsory schooling. When it comes to tertiary education, equity grounds lie behind calls for greater cost sharing. The argument, in brief, is that students receive substantial private benefits over their lifetimes, but bear a disproportionately small share of the costs. Thus, increases in fees and the substitution of loans for grants are seen as being equitable as well as helping to limit the public cost of the rising demand for places in tertiary education. Even where loan repayment is income contingent (not *all* tertiary graduates end up with above average incomes) many advocates of greater cost sharing also advocate a safety net of means-tested grants and scholarships for able but poor students, for whom higher costs would deter them from enrolling.

We also argue in subsequent chapters that equity considerations provide a rationale for government support of pre-school education and care and lifelong learning programmes to retrain older and/or poorly qualified workers. In the case of ECEC, efficiency and equity arguments both point in the same direction, but for older workers equity considerations may persuade governments to subsidise retraining even though conventional rate of return analysis would not justify doing so.

Notes

1. Turkey, Greece, New Zealand, Portugal, Denmark and Italy.

2. Initial estimates were prepared by the OECD Secretariat for the Education Ministerial Meeting in 1996. These were refined in OECD (1999) and in some of the individual country reports summarised in OECD (2000a).

3. Turkey and Mexico regularly are shown to have the most to achieve in order to reach median or good practice provision.

4. Throughout this paper we are treating lifelong learning expenditure as investments rather than current consumption. While it may be the case that there are some aspects of lifelong learning which are primarily consumption, some adult education courses which are essentially for leisure and social purposes, for example, these are likely to comprise a relatively small proportion of total lifelong learning expenditure.

5. See, for example, Chapter 2 in Layard, Mayhew and Owen (1994).

6. Risk and uncertainty could have been discussed as types of capital market failures in the sense that perfect capital markets would enable students and trainees to insure their future incomes. Standard insurance problems such as moral hazard and adverse selection discourage widespread availability of income insurance.

7. In addition less risk averse individuals are likely to have self-selected themselves into entrepreneurial occupations.

8. The worker's post-training wage is reduced irrespective of where he or she is employed, but supply is only increased to the extent that trainees are expected to be retained post-training.

9. Because, especially for full-time courses, the appropriate tax reduction to foregone earnings is the *average* tax rate while returns are reduced by the *marginal* tax rate. In almost any real world tax system average tax rates are less than marginal rates for most individuals contemplating lifelong learning investments.

10. Of course, if minimum wages or other labour market rigidities prevent trainees financing their training by low initial wages, there could be an inadequate supply of willing trainees. Whether the appropriate response is a training subsidy rather than addressing the original rigidity in the labour market is, of course, another question.

11. In the UK, for example, Industrial Training Boards, implementing the requirements of the Industrial Training Act, operated a levy (and grant) system from 1964 until 1982. Although the system was to a large extent abolished by the Conservative government, remnants remain; for example the Engineering Construction ITB retains the power to impose a training levy of 1.5% of the wage bill.

12. The extreme case is that of pure monopsony, where there is a single employer. All that is required for the argument in the text is that there is a wedge between the wage and

the marginal product; firms' ability to hire and retain labour depends on the wage they pay. This is consistent with a degree of competition between employers, ruled out by definition in the pure monopsony model.

13. Providing general training may also help in recruitment and retention of workers.

14. Under such circumstances Stevens (1994) has shown that it is also possible that firms and workers will respond by *over*-investing in firm-specific human capital; because such investments reduce mobility of workers this reduces the chance of outside firms capturing the benefits of transferable training for which they have not paid.

Chapter 4

Costs and Benefits

1. Introduction

How can evidence on the costs and benefits of existing education and training guide us in establishing the outline of an integrated lifelong learning strategy? Does this evidence point to ways of increasing the cost-effectiveness of learning at different stages of the life cycle?

What do we know about costs and benefits of existing educational and training programmes? Put simply, what works? Can we use the answers to these questions to highlight programmes that may be extended so as to play a fuller role in a strategic lifelong learning plan? Do the answers suggest where it may be possible to increase benefits or reduce costs to revitalise programmes that currently are regarded as not working? These are some of the issues dealt with in this chapter.

The approach is to focus more closely on lifelong learning issues, including funding, that occur at some specific stages of the life cycle. This is done in part for expositional convenience. As argued throughout this paper, one of the corollaries of the lifelong approach to learning is the necessity, when considering the net benefits of specific human capital investments, to consider interdependencies between such investments. In general, this implies that the returns to earlier investments are greater than returns to later investments because the productivity of the latter are augmented by the former. Conversely, the costs of correcting under-investment increase with the age of the individual. We will spell out these points in more detail below.

In this paper it is not possible to cover all lifelong learning related learning topics; the subject is simply too vast. Purely for reasons of brevity, this chapter pays somewhat less attention to the compulsory years of formal education, emphasising instead pre-school, upper secondary and tertiary education and to lifelong learning issues relevant to youth and adults not enrolled in formal education.[1] One reason for this is that enrolment in primary and lower secondary education is near-universal in OECD countries. This does not, of course mean that there are no relevant issues – there are and we touch on them below. A fuller study would pay more attention than we are able to here to quality and curriculum issues and to administrative/financial issues such as the respective roles of central and local governments at these levels of education.

As well as providing the context for sector specific discussion, the data should be read in conjunction with the description in Chapter 3 of the "participation gaps" methodology. Although we do not formally use that methodology in the current paper, these figures will give an idea of where such gaps may arise in each country that might wish to adopt a "good practice" methodology. Of course, this approach ignores qualitative aspects that are important to a successful lifelong learning strategy.

2. Early childhood education and care

a) *Empirical background*

Figure 8 demonstrates considerable variability across OECD countries in enrolments of young children in ECEC.

Figure 8. **Enrolment of children aged 2-4 as percentage of population aged 2-4 in public and private institutions (full-time and part-time), 1996**

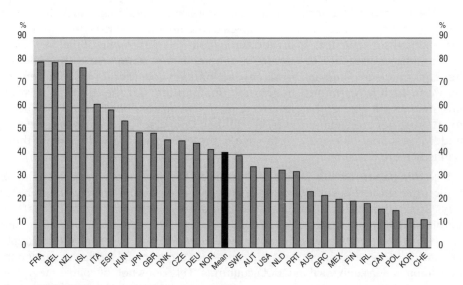

Source: OECD (1998).

Figure 9. **Expenditure on pre-primary education as a percentage of GDP, 1995**

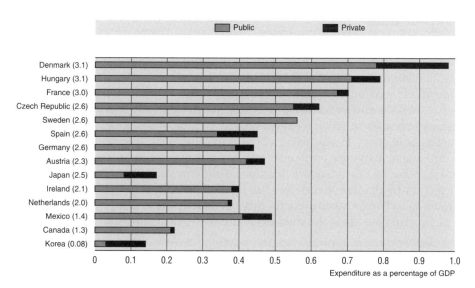

Note: The figures in parentheses give the average number of years in pre-primary education.
Source: OECD (1999).

Clearly some countries have wide coverage (Belgium, France, New Zealand and Iceland having nearly 80% of the age group enrolled, approximately twice the OECD average) while even some of the more affluent countries in the OECD (USA, Canada, Finland, Austria and the Netherlands) have under 40% enrolment. Of course this only captures institutional enrolment; informal early childhood and care is omitted. Clearly there are participation gaps (see Chapter 3, Section 2) to be filled in this sector by many countries. The figure is only intended to give some picture of the degree of cross-country variation. Many other dimensions of early childhood and care in particular amounts (measured say in hours per week) and quality are important.

Expenditure as a proportion of GDP also vary considerably, as Figure 9 shows for a selection of OECD countries. The figure also shows that this index is related quite closely to the average number of years in pre-primary education. The data on which the figure is based refer, as in the previous figure, to organised, centre-based instruction programmes, in this case primarily covering children aged three to compulsory school age. Again, many informal day-care programmes, play groups and home-based programmes are excluded. For further background data on early childhood and care see Verry (1998) and OECD (1999).

© OECD 2001

b) *Rationale for government subsidies for* ECEC

Market imperfections

One class of such imperfections relates to capital markets. If all parents could borrow against their own or even their children's future income at the same interest rate, investments in ECEC would not require current sacrifices and would not be dependent on parental income. But economists have noted repeatedly that, for reasons of moral hazard and adverse selection, human capital is poor collateral for those wishing to borrow to finance education and training. Risks of default are high for a number of reasons. In particular, where repayments are income-contingent moral hazard arises; earnings, and hence repayments, can be kept low by occupational choice and/or by labour supply decisions. Furthermore, if the debts have been contracted not by children themselves but by their parents, society may be unwilling to enforce collection on moral grounds; this argument is likely to apply with special force to ECEC, given the age of the child when its parents incur the debt.

With imperfect capital markets, parental investments in their children are likely to be constrained by family incomes and savings; thus the cost of resources invested in children varies across families. In these circumstances, even if parents took the full range of costs and benefits into account their investments would not, in aggregate, be efficient. Relaxation of borrowing constraints could, in principle, improve the allocation of resources. Whether this is best achieved by intervention in the capital market or by subsidising ECEC is not obvious. Nevertheless, the use of direct subsidies, tax credits and/or childcare vouchers has been supported on grounds of capital market imperfections in order to secure more efficient levels and patterns of investment in children.

Externalities

Even where capital markets do not constrain household investment decisions, efficient outcomes will not result if private decision-makers do not take into account the full range of costs and benefits when making decisions about their ECEC expenditure. Under such circumstances is it possible that ECEC provides benefits to society as a whole in excess of those accruing to the households demanding it? If so, this would again provide a rationale for government intervention in order to equate *social* rather than private costs and benefits at the margin. Note that the mere existence of positive externalities does not determine the *type* of intervention that deals most efficiently with the externality in question; regulation, tax credits or direct subsidies may all help to "internalise" externalities. What are the relevant externalities that society may reap with extended ECEC provision?

One of the externalities increasing the returns to ECEC derives from the synergy between early and later skill formation. As Heckman (1999) puts it: "Early learning begets later learning and early success breeds later success just as early failure breeds later failure." Thus, ECEC investment not only increases private returns (and hence the optimal amounts) of later human capital investment, but reduces unit costs in primary and secondary schooling by reducing repeating rates (grade retention) and increasing completion probabilities. If families fail to take account of these later effects society may under-invest in ECEC.

We examine below the evidence for other types of externalities relating to social outcomes as various as welfare recipiency, propensities to teen pregnancy and criminal behaviour (as measured say by arrest rates). Furthermore, there is good evidence that high quality ECEC programmes improve social skills and motivation, often ignored in academic studies in favour of examining programme effects on cognitive skills.

Informational failures

The above discussion has concentrated on two types of market failure: capital market imperfections and externalities. This is not an exhaustive list. Other types of failure could also generate a role for public policy. There may be information failures in the ECEC market. For example, families may be poorly informed about the effects on their children of different types and qualities of ECEC, about the range of suppliers or about the quality of service provided by suppliers they do know about. Under certain conditions (see Walker, 1991) these informational problems could be dealt with by publicly provided information on suppliers and/or by government regulation. Alternatively, subsidies selectively supporting high quality providers could induce and increase in the quality of ECEC purchased by parents.

Dynamic effects on government budgets

ECEC subsidies, by increasing labour force participation of parents, can assist low income households to free themselves from dependency on state benefits and achieve lasting economic self-sufficiency. Even if current ECEC subsidies for low income working parents were more expensive than current welfare support, the fact that employment increases human capital and reinforces work habits could generate long run savings in welfare in excess of the value of limited duration ECEC subsidies. This benefit of government subsidies is independent of the effects of ECEC subsidies on *children* and such subsidies tend not to restrict the type or quality of the childcare that can be purchased. This raises an issue which is perhaps under-researched in the ECEC literature: is there a trade-off between the policy goals of increasing the labour force participation of mothers and of improving child outcomes? Blau (2000) finds some evidence that there is. A subsidy designed specifically to achieve one of these goals will usually be relatively ineffective in achieving the other.

Equity and paternalism

Policy interventions may also be justified if state provided or subsidised ECEC would help to promote society's anti-poverty or equity goals. This would seem to be the implicit rationale for many programmes targeted on children in underprivileged backgrounds, such as Head Start in the United States. Without compensatory assistance, children from such backgrounds do not start their formal primary schooling on a level playing field with their peers from more privileged backgrounds. Without assistance not only are these children likely to experience inferior ECEC, at least from the point of view of being in a structured learning environment, but ECEC costs are a greater burden to their families than to wealthier families.

It can be argued that it is more cost-effective for an inequality averse government to attempt to equalise early endowments than to compensate for unequal outcomes later in life. Not only does early disadvantage beget later disadvantage, but evidence on adult training programmes suggests that it is more difficult to design effective programmes to compensate for cumulated disadvantage.

Certainly, in the United States and Great Britain, and probably in other OECD countries also, household surveys provide evidence of the regressive nature of such expenditure. For example, Casper (1995) using data from the Survey of Income and Programme Participation for 1993 discusses a number of dimensions of inequality in ECEC in the US. ECEC expenditure form a larger proportion of family income for low income families and for families below the poverty line than for wealthier families. It is likely that the inequality is even greater than such data indicate because higher income families may be expected, on average, to purchase higher quality ECEC; *i.e.* standardised for quality, the expenditure would be even more regressive. Putting the quality question aside, for the welfare-to-work and working poor populations childcare costs of the order of 25% of family earnings are likely to be significant barrier to employment for mothers in such families. Where the burden of providing ECEC is as unequal as this, governments seeking to ensure equality of opportunity and reduce the intergenerational transmission of inequality may well conclude that there is a *prima facie* case for subsidising low income families.

An alternative approach to targeting government assistance on equity and anti-poverty grounds is to direct such assistance to single parent households. Labour force participation is lower for single parents and, where single parents do work, their hours are shorter than are the hours of working parents in general. These factors place single parents and their children at risk of having low income, even of falling into poverty. To the extent that young children prevent lone parents from working on the one hand, and that increased labour force participation, and increased hours of participants, offer an escape route from low income and poverty for single parent households on the other, the equity case for targeting ECEC assistance to lone parents is compelling.

Furthermore, given the vital importance of ECEC as a foundation for later learning and development, the case for paternalism is probably stronger for very young children than later in the life cycle. Dysfunctional families and inimical social environments can do lasting damage, and many would argue that early intervention to offset these disadvantages may be justified on paternalistic grounds if not on others. Although it may be possible, and this is by no means certain, to remedy later in life some of the adverse consequences of inadequate early investments, the later such remediation is left the more costly it is likely to be.

c)   Private and social benefits of ECEC: evidence

Recent research, which has largely been conducted in the US (although OECD, 1999, cites studies conducted in other OECD countries) demonstrates the importance of skill formation in early pre-school years during which family and other non-institutional environments shape abilities and motivation. Here we present a very selective example of the type of evidence that has been adducted.

One of the most studied high quality ECEC programmes in the US is the Perry Preschool Program.[2] Some results from this programme are presented in Table 7. First, raw differences between the experimental (programme) group and the control group are shown. Second, some benefit-cost figures from the project are reproduced and discussed.

The table would seem to show clear differences between the groups in educational, economic and social dimensions. Note that because these benefits are measured at age 27 they measure persistent benefits (in fact in the whole study, evidence that pre-school benefits are transitory only exists for gains in childhood intelligence test scores). The pre-school programme would appear to have had beneficial effects on its subjects. This does not mean that the project was "worthwhile" in an economic sense. To know whether that is indeed the case two further steps are required; the benefits have to be given monetary values, and the sum of these has to be compared with the costs of the programme.

An attempt to do such cost-benefit calculations was made based on the information available when the subject and control groups were aged 19 and 27. Table 8 (from Edward Gramlich's commentary in Berrueta-Clement et al., 1984) shows the benefits and costs, shown separately for participants and the rest of society, on the basis of data collected when participants were age 19 having spent one year in the Perry Preschool programme.

61

Table 7. **Some major findings from the Perry Preschool Study**

Panel 7*a*. Educational benefits (measured at age 19 unless otherwise specified)

Percentage (unless stated otherwise)

		Experimental group	Control group
1	Average or better literacy	61	38
2	High school graduate or equivalent	67	49
3	Percentage of years in special education	16	28
4	Mean high school GPA (A = 4, B = 3....)	2.09	1.68
5	Reading achievement (age 14)	31.5	21.7
6	Arithmetic achievement (age 14)	31.5	25.0
7	Language achievement (age 14)	46.5	34.8

Note: Rows 5-7 are raw scores from the California Achievement Tests. All group differences are significant at $p < 0.05$ (two-tailed): to say that the differences are significant at the 0.05 level means that they would occur by chance no more than 5 times out of 100.

Panel 7*b*. Economic benefits (measured at age 27)

Percentage (unless stated otherwise)

		Experimental group	Control group
1	$2 000 or more monthly earnings	29	7
2	Mean annual earnings	$13 328	$11 186
3	Currently employed	71	59
4	Month unemployed in previous 2 years	5.7	8.0
5	Homeowner at age 27	36	13

Note: Group differences are significant at $p < 0.05$ (two-tailed), except row 2 ($p = 0.069$), row 3 ($p = 0.181$) and row 4 ($p = 0.289$).

Panel 7*c*. Social benefits (measured at age 27 unless otherwise stated)

Percentage (unless stated otherwise)

		Experimental group	Control group
1	Ever detained or arrested (age 19)	31	51
2	5 or more arrests by age 27	7	35
3	Received social services in past 10 years	59	80
4	Pregnant during teen years (% of females)	48	67
5	Mother during teen years (% of females)	44	54

Source: Berrueta-Clement *et al.* (1984); Schweinhart (1993).

Schweinhart (1993) conducts a similar analysis on the basis of observing the experimental and control groups at age 27. Looking just at the net present value and the benefit/cost ratio the author derives the following figures in Table 9.

Table 8.   **Per-child benefits (+) and costs (–) of one year participation in the Perry Preschool Programme**

1981 US$, present values (discounted at 3%)

	Programme participants (and families) (1)	Taxpayers and potential crime victims (2)	Society (1) + (2)
Measured benefits (+) and costs (–), to age 19			
Operating and capital costs			
of preschool programme	0	–4 818	–4 818
Child care	290	0	290
Educational cost saving	0	5 113	5 113
Earnings increases	482	161	643
Welfare reduction	–546	601	55
Crime reduction	0	1 233	1 233
Subtotal	226	2 290	2 516
Predicted (+) and costs (–), age 19+			
College costs	0	–704	–704
Earnings gain	19 233	4 580	23 813
Reduction in welfare			
Payments	–14 377	15 815	1 438
Crime reduction	0	1 871	1 871
Subtotal	4 856	21 562	26 418
Total (net present value)	5 082	23 852	28 933
Benefit/cost ratio	1.34	5.32	6.24

Source: Berrueta-Clement *et al.* (1984).

Table 9.   **Benefits and costs of the Perry Preschool Programme, age 27**

	Programme participants (and families) (1)	Taxpayers and potential crime victims (2)	Society (1) + (2)
Net present value (1992 US$)	19 570	76 077	95 646
Benefit/cost ratio	8.38	6.75	8.23

Source: Schweinhart (1993).

Naturally, there is much that can be disputed in the way the benefits of the programme have been measured (readers are referred to the original sources for details). Furthermore, major uncertainty must attach to the projected earnings differentials and crime reductions over the remainder of the working life from age 19 (or 27). Nevertheless, these figures do indicate such large net gains (and high benefit/cost ratios) that even if the benefits are substantially overestimated it seems

63

unlikely that the project would not be worthwhile in net present value terms. It is also interesting to note how much larger the net present value is to the "taxpayer and potential crime victims group" compared to the value to participants in the pre-school programme itself. This could be interpreted as providing *a priori* grounds for governments to subsidise such projects.

It *does* seem to be the case that the more intensive, longer and higher cost per child programmes such as the Perry and the Syracuse Preschool Scheme have larger and longer lasting effects than the more universal and cheaper programmes such as Head Start, which has shorter periods of intervention, lower paid staff and limited parental involvement.

It also seems to be the case that targeted programmes, carefully designed to meet the needs of the target group, are likely to be good investments. But it is extremely difficult to extrapolate the results of such studies to different groups in different circumstances. For example, while one may accept the positive findings reported for the Perry Preschool Programme, we are not justified in using these findings to underpin more general expansion of ECEC to the whole population of pre-schoolers. For one thing, the sample sizes of the Perry experimental and control groups are just too small. For another, the programme, perfectly understandably, was targeted at very disadvantaged children. The gains, both to participants and society at large, that were observed in the programme evaluation may not apply to a project which expands provision of ECEC to less disadvantaged children (unlikely, simply on a statistical basis to be involved in truancy, delinquency and crime to the same extent). Barnett (1995) cites evidence that age of entry to, or years of experience in, day care during pre-school years influenced early test scores (ages 5 and 6) differently for children from and high and low income homes. Early entry and/or more years in care had positive effects on scores from children from poor homes but *negative* effects for children in the highest income families. A possible explanation is that where the home environment is particularly conducive to cognitive development children will do worse outside the home, whereas children from home environments that are less supportive gain most from ECEC outside the home. If this is true it has obvious implications for the ability to extrapolate results from programmes for disadvantaged children to a more typically heterogeneous population. In general, we do not know to what extent the results from expensive high quality model programmes targeted at specific population groups would generalise to larger scale programmes which are less specifically targeted and would in all probability have to operate with fewer resources per child than the model programmes. To what extent would slightly lower quality programmes generate positive but proportionately lower benefits? Is the relationship between size and effectiveness non-linear; *i.e.* is there some quality threshold below which benefits fall away sharply?

Probably our best evidence of large scale ECEC programmes comes from the US Head Start programme. Although targeted at disadvantaged children, Head Start is much larger than most model programmes, enrolling about 800 000 children in 1999, although even this number only constitutes about 35% of eligible three and four year-olds. Evaluations of Head Start and other ECEC programmes are summarised in Currie (2001). She finds that Head Start, in spite of variations in quality across different centres, is associated with short-term gains in cognitive skills as well as longer term gains in school completion. Head Start helps children avoid grade repetition and placement in special track education. However, evaluations also suggest that some of these gains are subject to "fadeout"; the gains in cognitive test scores, for example, begin to disappear by the time the children reach third grade. There is some suggestion that fadeout is greatest for children whose post-ECEC is of poor quality and is not, therefore, inevitable. Currie estimates that the short- and medium-term benefits of Head Start offset between 40% and 60% of programme costs. Longer term benefits have not been evaluated, but she argues that "even relatively small long-term benefits of such a programme may be sufficient to offset the costs of public investment". The Perry evaluation suggests that such long-term benefits are likely to be substantial.

Furthermore, as noted above the experimental design, which compares outcomes for the programme group and the control group, is unable to identify separate contributions of the different components of the Perry programme to its overall success.[3] One possible exception is the curriculum component. There is some evidence that children who follow the High/Scope active learning curriculum perform better on academic tests and have superior social and behavioural characteristics than children following alternative curricula (Weikart and Schweinhart, 1991).

d) Financing implications

One of the implications of the US findings is that high quality ECEC programmes of kind where net benefits, private and social, have been clearly established, do not come cheaply. There are several reasons for this but, in essence, such programmes rely on high staff/child ratios and utilise highly trained staff.

When we discuss tertiary education funding we will be advocating reforms involving a greater degree of cost sharing than most countries generally adopt. Can similar arguments be made in the case of ECEC? Probably not. One means of cost sharing is to persuade parents to remain at home with their children in the early years. But this runs counter to one of the main benefits of ECEC – allowing greater labour force participation for mothers and reducing welfare dependency. Some countries place so much weight on these latter objectives that the receipt or level of ECEC subsidies are conditional on labour force participation. In Germany and Sweden policy is less biased to parental participation, acknowledging both the benefits of parental care and the cost saving it generates. Even where parents take a greater share of ECEC responsibility, complementary programmes (parental education, centre-based sessions to provide socialisation, etc.) will incur substantial costs.

As in all sectors, there will be scope in ECEC for using existing resources more effectively (avoiding duplication of services, identifying "dormant" resources such as unused buildings, exploiting voluntary labour, etc.). Nevertheless, a major expansion of ECEC in terms of both quantity and quality will certainly require the mobilisation of additional resources. There is some scope for utilising the tax system to provide incentives for employers to take a greater role in ECEC provision as well as offering more generous parental leave. Of course, if firms are forced to expand their provision, there will exist some uncertainty as to the final incidence of the ECEC costs they incur; they could be passed on in terms of higher prices, lower wages or minimised by discriminatory hiring policies. Tax incentives may also be used to leverage funds from the voluntary sector and to encourage private start-ups in ECEC provision.

In terms of equity goals, any cost recovery from public supply, and subsidised use of privately provided ECEC, needs to guard against low income parents having access only to low quality ECEC, often purely custodial, while more affluent parents are able to afford higher quality more structured programmes. The Perry Programme and to a lesser extent Head Start in the US show that children from disadvantaged backgrounds benefit enormously from high quality ECEC.

Most countries do charge parents fees in publicly provided ECEC. Often these are means tested, and in terms of equity this is sensible where universal subsidisation is too expensive. Of course this can impose high implicit marginal tax rates on households as income increases. There is also a growing use of attendance related fees. Again, this is sensible in terms of cost-recovery but can induce poorer households to limit their use of publicly provided services.

e) ECEC: *Summary and crucial policy issues*

The analysis in this section supports the view that ECEC investments provide a good social return; there are compelling efficiency and equity arguments for governments to provide as wide as possible access to high quality ECEC. However, as in other areas of lifelong learning, funds are limited. Furthermore, we argued that the case for cost sharing may be less compelling than for other components of lifelong learning. In such circumstances it probably makes more sense to expand the coverage of programmes for disadvantaged children (*i.e.* to target low income and single parent households), for whom the evidence of high net returns is strongest, than to aim for universal coverage.

Apart from the issue of universality versus selectivity in the provision of ECEC, a number of pedagogical issues need to be considered as part of a lifelong learning strategy. One of these is the balance between cognitive and non-cognitive components in ECEC programmes. For example, some Head Start evaluations have argued for greater emphasis on academic goals such as reading readiness (or, more generally, school readiness) and general language and literacy skills. However, this is not to deny the importance of non-cognitive skills; the question of the actual content of ECEC programmes is a subtle one and does not lend itself to easy generalisation.

Another issue is the *optimal age for intervention*. Some recent brain research,[4] aided by advances in brain imaging technology, has highlighted the first three years as critical for brain growth. Some of this research suggests the rapid growth of the brain in these early years provides the opportunity for learning arrangements to play a part in its development, actually influencing circuit development. However, it would probably be premature to conclude that public policy should give higher priority to ages birth to three- than to four- and five-year-old pre-schoolers, nor that interventions directed at this group come too late. Demonstrating that the first three years are important in brain development is not the same as proving that extra stimulation in specific learning environments produces lasting benefits for normal children. The US National Research Council (2001) has recently concluded that "It is important (...) to caution against thinking that brain research is directly applicable to instruction and pedagogy. There are many popular accounts and heavily promoted learning programmes that make that leap, but so far, there is no evidence of the effectiveness of particular educational programmes, methods, or techniques on brain development".

The cost per child of ECEC depends on the quality of provision. Because of the diverse nature of ECEC it is difficult to be precise about what constitutes a high quality pre-school programme. Certain structural dimensions of quality are relatively easily measurable; child-adult ratios, class size, teacher experience and qualifications. Less easily quantifiable are "process" factors such as the nature of adult-child interactions, the cognitive stimulation children receive, etc.[5] Due to high variation in the quality of existing provision, information asymmetries between parents and providers and the harmful potential of poor quality ECEC, governments need to consider whether quality is best ensured by state provision, government regulation of private providers or a mix of the two.

Even accepting the economic and educational arguments for making ECEC a high priority in an overall lifelong learning strategy, resources will be scarce; every effort should be made to ensure cost-effectiveness, to recover costs from more affluent households, and to mobilise resources from social partners. In spite of these efforts, increased public funding of ECEC will probably be necessary, especially in those OECD countries where current provision leaves substantial gaps in participation or where coverage for low income households is essentially custodial.

3. Primary and secondary schooling

In these sectors, at least up until the early to mid-teens, participation in OECD countries is near-universal so, as argued in the introduction to this section, the emphasis of reforms relevant to lifelong learning is likely to be on quality and cost-effectiveness.

In Chapter 2 we adduced evidence indicating that the compulsory sector in many OECD countries may not be performing as effectively as many would like, especially as students receiving schooling in the compulsory sector have their direct costs fully subsidised. This evidence was of two types: firstly, evidence coming from international comparisons of student achievement and, secondly, evidence indicating the existence of high levels of adult illiteracy even in countries with high levels of educational participation. These skill gaps must in part reflect failures of the school system, although undoubtedly family background factors also contribute significantly. They imply the need to target illiteracy and, more generally, to improve the quality of learning for lower ability children.

There is now a large body of evidence, mainly produced in and relating to the United States, about the effects of primary and secondary spending per pupil, teacher salaries, class size and material inputs on educational and economic outcomes. The weight of the findings suggests that money spent on improving these commonly used indices of school quality is, at best, likely to have very uncertain results. One possible reading of the evidence suggests that such expenditure are generally not cost-effective.

Some of this research attempts to relate expenditure per pupil, class size or other presumed quality indicators to test scores, while another body of literature relates them to the subsequent earnings of pupils. In both dimensions, the results are inconclusive. Surveys by Hanushek (1986, 1996) and analysis by Heckman *et al.* (1996, 1997) either fail to find clear positive effects of increased spending or demonstrate that positive effects depend crucially on *ad hoc* assumptions. Heckman *et al.* (1997) show, for US high schools, increasing spending per student by 10% produces negative net discounted returns using the largest rates of return to labour market earnings found in the literature. Card and Krueger (1996), while acknowledging that some results are not robust, take a slightly more optimistic view of the effects of increased spending, while the results of the Tennessee Star experiment finds a clear negative relationship between class size and test scores (Krueger, 1999; Krueger and Whitmore, 2001). Whether such results would generalise to a wider population in a non-experimental setting is not clear. Of course, at very low quality levels increases in per pupil expenditure, class size and teacher salaries may have a much larger effect on quality than the typical US finding (see Behrman and Birdsall, 1983). But marginal increases in expenditure at current levels of school quality in many OECD countries are not likely to be cost-effective policy.

This is not to say that nothing can be done to improve primary and secondary school quality. Curriculum reform, identification and widespread adoption of best-practice teaching techniques, the use of "literacy hours" and other remedial devices may all be effective. More fundamentally, casual observation suggests that in many countries young people have less self-discipline and are less motivated than their predecessors. Teachers and parents would probably agree that reviving and strengthening the learning culture among children and youth could transform schools. Unfortunately there is little certainty about how this can be achieved.

While surely not a comprehensive solution to such problems of culture and motivation, it is worth mentioning a genre of creative programmes targeted at adolescents from disadvantaged backgrounds who are still enrolled in formal schooling. Again most evaluation of these relates to the US. One class of such interventions is *mentoring programmes*. The Big Brothers/Big Sisters (BB/BS) programme pairs adult volunteers with adolescents from single-parent households while Philadelphia's Sponsor-a-Scholar (SAS) programme provides long-term mentoring throughout high school and one year beyond. This programme, unlike BB/BS, which offers broad support and friendship, is carefully structured to increase the chances of participant's progress from secondary schooling to college. Indeed, in addition to mentoring, SAS provides financial assistance for participants who enrol in an approved tertiary institution. The Quantum Opportunity Programme (QOP) offered financial incentives and mentoring for participation in programmes aimed at improving both social skills and market readiness. Other programmes have been targeted at teenage parents, encouraging them to stay in school. Evaluations of these programmes cited in Heckman (1999) show that they have clear benefits both in terms of schooling outcomes (grade point averages, reduced truancy, college attendance) and social skills (reduced drug and alcohol use, less aggressive behaviour, better relationship with parents).

4. Upper secondary and school to work transition

a) Empirical background

Because of the wide range of ages and activities covered by upper secondary and school to work transition, we approach the task of providing an empirical background from two perspectives. The next figures consider actual enrolments in formal education for young people. Between the ages of 17 and 20 young people still enrolled in education are shifting from secondary to post-secondary education so looking at either one will not give an accurate picture of how countries differ in their ability to retain young people in the education system. Therefore, Figures 10 to 13 show enrolment rates both in secondary and other educational levels for the ages 17 through 20. At age 17, most enrolment is in secondary schooling (Australia and

69

Figure 10. **Net secondary and total enrolment rates of 17-year-olds in public and private institutions, 1996**

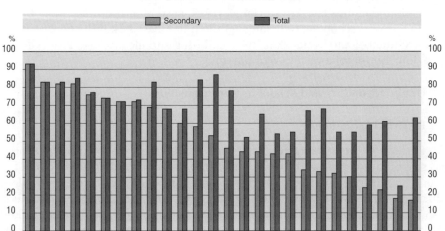

Note: Ranked in descending order of secondary enrolment rates.
Source: OECD (1998).

Figure 11. **Net secondary and total enrolment rates of 18-year-olds in public and private institutions, 1996**

Note: Ranked in descending order of secondary enrolment rates.
Source: OECD (1998).

Figure 12.   **Net secondary and total enrolment rates of 19-year-olds in public and private institutions, 1996**

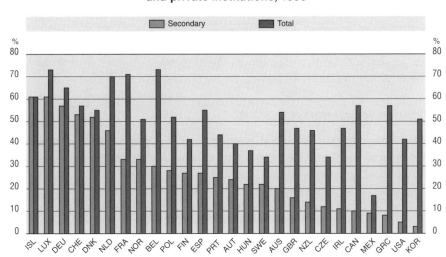

Note: Ranked in descending order of secondary enrolment rates.
Source: OECD (1998).

Figure 13.   **Net secondary and total enrolment rates of 20-year-olds in public and private institutions, 1996**

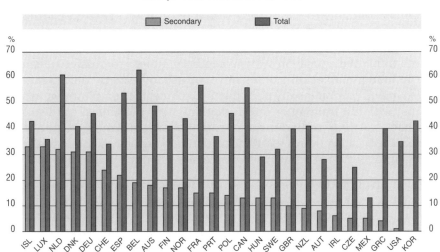

Note: Ranked in descending order of secondary enrolment rates.
Source: OECD (1998).

Canada have significant non-secondary enrolments) while by age 20 non-secondary education dominates enrolments. However, the proportion of 19- and 20-year-olds still enrolled in secondary education in some countries is noteworthy. Again these figures show wide variation across countries. Some countries have serious difficulties in retaining young people in formal education after compulsory schooling ends, while for a substantial group of countries the enrolment rate is 90% or above. Below we discuss further the trend for staying longer in school in some countries.

b) Objectives and approaches to reform

Within the OECD it is probably fair to say that the Nordic countries have devoted most thought and effort to school to work transition problems. For example, the general approach of guaranteeing to all young people up to the age of 18 or 20 a place in either education or training or work has been developed over two decades and has more recently been emulated, for example, in elements of the New Deal in the UK. These countries have also made strenuous efforts to involve employers and trade unions in programme design and certification. For young people, particularly those under 20, these countries have been successful in keeping students in school for longer than in many OECD countries. For those in their early to mid-twenties, although increasing numbers in this age bracket are still enrolled in upper secondary education in the Nordic countries, a combination of financial incentives and penalties within the welfare system is used to encourage them to enter employment or training.

Although almost all OECD countries have devoted substantial proportions of their welfare budgets to supporting young people who have been relatively unsuccessful in compulsory schooling, and have no realistic prospects in tertiary education, the lifelong learning approach suggests that improving skills and competences within the education system is to be preferred to passive welfare support. The labour market difficulties of young school leavers, which range from unemployment, predominantly part-time employment, or employment in "dead-end jobs" with few training or career development prospects, can usually be traced back to failure or under-achievement at school. Young people without sound basic education (which today includes IT and arguably some competence in foreign language) are not attractive to employers in today's labour market.

So the first objective of reform must be to address the issues of failure and underachievement in secondary schools, as well as early leaving. We discussed above the difficulties of knowing exactly how to achieve improved performance in secondary schooling but also considered some promising approaches. Our discussion of ECEC also suggests that subsequent failure and underachievement may be rooted in the early years of child development, implying that an effective indirect approach is to improve the quantity and quality of ECEC provision.

Policies to improve achievement in secondary schooling should also help in retaining students in the educational system. To achieve both goals it is necessary to confront the problems of low educational expectations and to work to instil greater awareness of the benefits of staying on. There may be, in addition, purely financial reasons for early leaving where students come from low income households which are unable to incur the opportunity cost of foregoing labour market earnings. As the young people in question will come from relatively disadvantaged backgrounds, and because we know that early leaving will, for many, result in lower lifetime earnings, there are strong equity arguments for devoting resources to increasing the staying on rate.

Reform of school to work pathways is predicated on the notion that it is undesirable and unnatural to treat learning and work as separate universes; to do so makes the transition from one to the other more difficult. Upper secondary schooling, in particular, but also tertiary education to some extent needs to address issues of integrating learning and work, while not becoming too narrowly vocational (which would make graduates from formal education institutions vulnerable down the line when job requirements change, as they are certain to do). Formal education needs to provide foundations on which more specifically job-oriented labour market training can build. It is sensible to have a division of labour, but educational institutions need to be sensitive to the way labour markets are evolving. Of course many OECD countries are already grappling with these issues and we will refer to some examples of what would appear to be good practice.

Apprenticeships

Although apprenticeships are also important in Australia, Austria, Norway, the UK and the US, the basic model still held up for possible emulation is the German apprenticeship system. Certainly, the evidence suggests that German youth have benefited from the system (as evidenced, for example by the fact that Germany has consistently had lower youth unemployment than OECD or EU average rates). The German system appears to suffer less from the Achilles Heel of most such schemes, namely that they are regarded as second class by young people, their parents and even employers. This system has succeeded in motivating students to do well in order to secure desirable apprenticeships and inducing firms to provide training opportunities and in doing so has broken down artificial barriers between the worlds of work and learning. Nevertheless, even in Germany (and other countries with traditional apprenticeship schemes), there has been some falling off in their popularity, both among young people who appear to be put off by the difficulty of transferring into tertiary education, and with firms which have been more reluctant to offer apprenticeships as the German economy has encountered (relative to its "miracle years") difficult conditions. Finally there is a growing recognition that the German system cannot simply be transferred to other countries.

73

The institutional foundations, forms of social partnership and levels of government regulation which have enabled the German system to succeed do not exist in all countries which might wish to adopt a German style apprenticeship system.

Financial support to prevent early school leaving

This can be attempted by a number of policy instruments. Maintenance grants for upper secondary pupils are one possibility. Sweden and Norway have study grants available to different types of student, and Austria also has means tested grants for able students. Other countries (Austria, Finland) have accommodation allowances for students who have to board. Scholarships for needy and able students (Japan), and extending loan systems to secondary schooling (Finland, Japan, Norway) are other methods currently in use.

The use of loans (even where there is an element of subsidy) raises the question of cost sharing at the upper secondary level. While in most countries upper secondary is free at point of delivery (capital and recurrent costs met by state) and other countries provide maintenance support as well, the pattern is not universal. In Japan and South Korea many upper secondary schools charge fees. While increasing overall resources in the upper secondary sector, there has been a price to be paid in terms of equity as high quality upper secondary education has become beyond the resources of some low income families, although, as noted above, this consequence is ameliorated by the use of scholarships. Where apprenticeship schemes exist both firms and pupils contribute directly or indirectly to the costs.

Upper secondary schooling is probably the area where equity and efficiency considerations are most in conflict. As noted, where a decent upper secondary education has become a prerequisite for the acquisition of "good jobs" and access to further education, the equity argument for public funding is really no different than for compulsory schooling. Nevertheless, the fact that individuals themselves reap private benefits (in terms of access to higher education and directly in terms of labour market earnings) and their employers benefit by having access to more highly trained potential employees, there is some case to be made for an element of cost sharing.

Qualifications and curriculum

We discuss later in this chapter, as part of our discussion of how to increase returns to lifelong learning, the need to make qualifications more portable across education types and sectors. Essentially, what is required is double qualification pathways which can provide access to tertiary education and meet job market requirements. Typically such qualifications will involve an element of job experience; apprenticeships, internships and student work projects have all been suggested.

Such pathways may also confer an externality in that by linking work and learning more closely they make students more inclined to seek learning opportunities throughout their working lives.

5. Tertiary education

a) Access and funding: background

In most OECD countries tertiary education is no longer an elite activity. Large proportions of the age group are enrolled, and there is near parity in enrolment by gender. Nevertheless, within this overall picture there remain substantial differences across countries in proportions of the age groups enrolled in tertiary education as Figures 14-16 show. For example, for 18-21 year-olds enrolment rates in non-university and university tertiary education vary from over 40% to under 10% of the age group with the standard deviation being exactly one half the mean value.

Once again we observe substantial cross-country variation in enrolments across countries. For 18-21 year-olds, low tertiary enrolment may reflect the fact that substantial numbers are still in secondary schooling. Thus, although Denmark has low tertiary enrolments of 18-21 year-olds (under 10%) we recall that over 50%

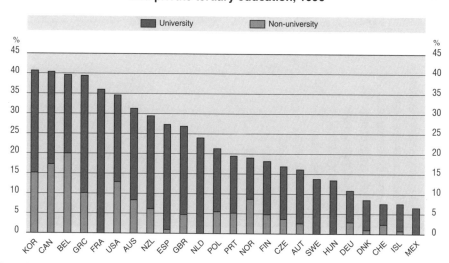

Figure 14. **Net enrolment rates for 18-21 year-olds in public and private tertiary education, 1996**

Note: Where no non-university enrolment is shown, the category is inappropriate or the data do not distinguish between university and non-university tertiary.
Source: OECD (1998).

Figure 15. **Net enrolment rates for 22-25 year-olds in public and private tertiary education, 1996**

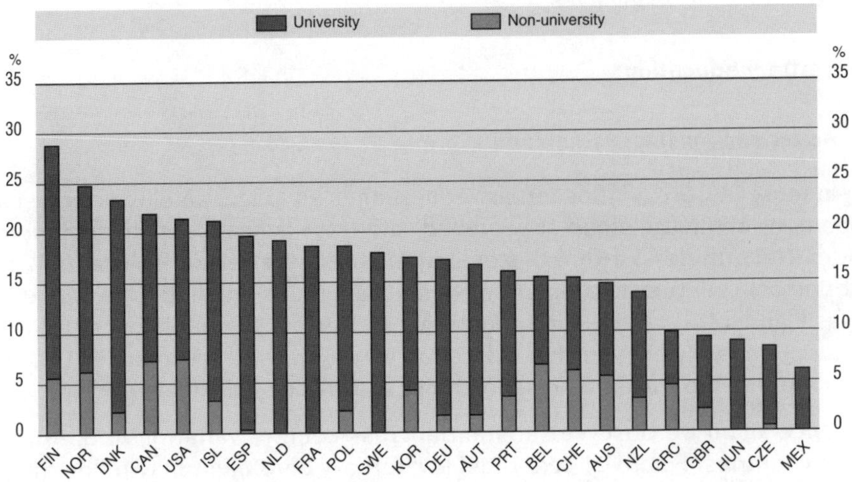

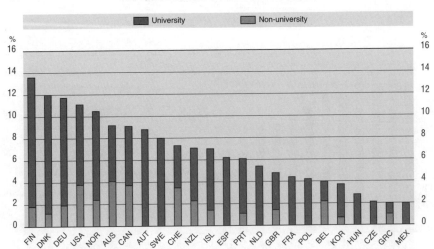

Note: Where no non-university enrolment is shown, the category is inappropriate or the data do not distinguish between university and non-university tertiary.
Source: OECD (1998).

Figure 16. **Net enrolment rates for 26-29 year-olds in public and private tertiary education, 1996**

Note: Where no non-university enrolment is shown, the category is inappropriate or the data do not distinguish between university and non-universtiy tertiary.
Source: OECD (1998).

of Danish 19-year-olds are still enrolled in secondary education and over 30% of 20-year-olds. When we look at tertiary enrolments for ages 22-25 Denmark has the third highest figure (nearly one-quarter of the age group). These difficulties of interpretation notwithstanding, the figures show large cross-country differences in tertiary enrolments.

Enrolment figures reflect both participation rates and the length of time people spend in tertiary education. Figure 17 shows, perhaps more clearly, the extent to which countries differ in the tertiary education received by young people; it shows the expected years of tertiary education for all 17-year-olds.[6] On average, across OECD countries, this turns out to be 2.33 years. Again, the variation is substantial; in Canada and the US the average 17-year-old expects to complete nearly four years of tertiary education while for a large group of OECD countries, including the UK, Sweden, Denmark, Austria, Greece and Germany, the expectation is less than half that while in the Czech Republic and Mexico the expectation is only about one year. Another notable feature is that countries where the expected years of tertiary education are greatest tend to be the countries where non-university education is important relative to university education. Countries that are able to offer a greater variety of types and durations in general succeed in providing their young people with more tertiary education.

Figure 17. **Expected years of tertiary education for all 17-year-olds, 1996**

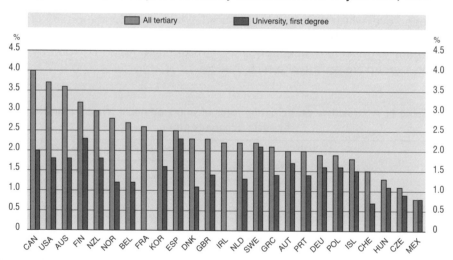

Note: No distinction is made between full-time and part-time years. Expected years depend on the duration of tertiary studies as well as participation rates.
Source: OECD (1998).

77

What the figures conceal is that within all OECD countries, albeit to different extents, participation is heavily dependent on family income and other socio-economic indicators. Table 10 documents this inequality in Britain, by way of example.

Table 10.   **Unequal access to higher education in Great Britain**

Socio-economic group	Participation rates in higher education (1997/98)	Percentage shares of university entrance (1999)
Professional	80	13.4
Intermediate	49	39.0
Skilled non-manual	32	12.0
Skilled manual	19	14.4
Partly skilled	18	7.4
Unskilled	14	1.7
Unknown		12.1
All	34	100.0

Source: Greenaway and Haynes (2000).

Nor, in general, is there a pronounced trend towards greater equality as Table 11 illustrates for selected countries. Only in the US have participation rates of the low socio-economic groups grown faster than the average growth rate. Even here it is difficult to be absolutely sure that the data do establish this trend. High year-to-year fluctuations in US participation rates make growth rates sensitive to the period over which the trend is measured. While changing the period of analysis and/or using moving averages does not affect the broad conclusion that only in the US do we observe falling inequality, growth rates of participation by socio-economic group are sensitive to such changes.

Table 11.   **Growth in participation rates of young adults in tertiary education by socio-economic group**

	Years covered	Annual average percentage change	
		Total	Low socio-economic group
Belgium	1985-1992	1.6	0.7
France	1982-1993	1.2	0.6
Ireland	1986-1992	1.8	1.5
Japan	1990-1996	1.0	0.6
United Kingdom	1991-1997	1.8	1.0
Unites States	1990-1996	0.9	1.2

Source: OECD (1999).

Outside the US the pattern of participation by socio-economic background has not changed greatly. If anything, as the table shows, inequality has increased.

In terms of sources of funding a wide variety of funding schemes exist, and we do not even attempt to summarise them here. To give a broad indication of the diversity, Figure 18 shows the proportion of public and private funding of tertiary education in 1997.

Figure 18.   **Distribution of public and private sources of funds for tertiary education institutions, 1997**

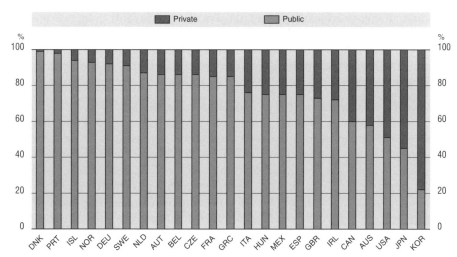

Source: OECD (2000).

While on average just over three quarters of tertiary educational funding is public, there is wide variation. In the Scandinavian countries, Portugal, Iceland and Germany over 90% of tertiary funding is public; in Australia, North America, Japan and Korea 40% or more of total funding is private. Currently, the mix of government funding and the fee contribution made by students varies quite substantially across OECD countries. In Japan and Korea students make substantial contributions (given the preponderance of private universities). In Sweden and the Czech Republic, there are still no fees in higher education institutions, while in Holland fee income only accounts for 6% of university funding. Other countries, such as the UK, may be said to be in a transitional phase where the proportion of funding derived from fees has recently increased and the possibility of still further increases is being actively, and sometimes vituperatively, debated.

b) Access and funding: reform

Most OECD governments subscribe to the goal of accelerating the process of transforming participation in tertiary education from an elite to a mass activity. Given the large (and growing) private economic benefits of such participation, extending access is a relatively uncontroversial objective. At the same time, increases in private returns have strengthened incentives both to the traditional tertiary intake and adults without higher education to enrol. Enrolment rates in tertiary education in the OECD rose by an average of 40% in the first half of the 1990s (OECD, 1999) including a growing number entering in their late twenties or older, either because they missed out when they were younger or coming back for additional higher education. The numbers of such "second chancers" and "second biters" can be expected to grow in the future if a lifelong learning culture really takes hold in the adult population. Improved upper secondary completion rates, and, in some countries, growth in the relative size of the tertiary-aged cohort, have reinforced the increased private demand.

However, it is not clear that governments have thought through the funding implications of meeting increased demand. Can major expansions and extending access to currently underrepresented socio-economic groups be financed from general taxation, given other demands on the public purse and pressures to contain or reduce public expenditure relative to national income? Where the answer is in the negative, two possibilities exist, given that governments are also concerned not to allow major deterioration in the quality of higher education. The first is to seek efficiency savings (productivity gains). If these are substantial it is conceivable that existing funding levels could support higher enrolments. In the UK, for example, real funding *per student* declined by about 50% in real terms over last 20 years. At the same time, regulation has increased dramatically and accountability reviews have proliferated. Arguably, all this has led to increased productivity (the austerity measures and increased workloads have even led to limited adoption of new technologies in traditional universities, normally somewhat resistant to technical change), but many would question this. There is no doubt that student-staff ratios and class sizes have increased. Academics report that they work harder while their pay has fallen relative to comparable non-manual groups and to academic pay abroad (in the US especially). Efficiency probably has increased but there can be little doubt that continuation of these trends will eventually affect the quality of teaching and research and create problems for the hiring and retention of academic staff of the highest calibre.[7] This makes the second option, reform of financing mechanisms, a high priority.

In the context of this paper, reform of the financing of tertiary education is seen as freeing up some public funds and thus contributing to the overall resources available to be spread across the many initiatives that a comprehensive lifelong learning strategy entails. Within the context of tertiary education, additional objectives of reform include (Greenaway and Haynes, 2000):

- Reducing social exclusion.

- Enhancing the resource base of tertiary education.

- Promoting greater diversity and innovation among educational providers.

- Increasing efficiency in provision.

Many proposals for the reform of tertiary funding exist. These include graduate taxes, vouchers and income-contingent loans. All have their merits and shortcomings. We do not advocate vouchers here. Although they may generate greater efficiency by distributing public funds to individuals rather than institutions (which would then face competition and become more responsive to "consumer demand") vouchers do not, in themselves, generate additional resources.

So, to achieve the triple aim of reducing the public input into tertiary education, expanding access to the system and maintaining or improving quality, additional private funds must be mobilised to supplement and to some extent replace public expenditure. Greater cost sharing is required. While some extra contributions will continue to come from the families of students, over-reliance on this source will perpetuate the current patterns of unequal participation in higher education. Reform of tertiary finance consistent with achieving the objectives above is likely to involve two additional elements:

- *Greater fee differentiation* between institutions to reflect their different locations and mix of activities, between subjects to reflect their different costs and between students to reflect their different backgrounds. In the US, with a large private sector fee differentiation has existed for many years. Other OECD countries have recently introduced differentiation in some dimensions, for example in Australia tertiary fees vary by subject. In New Zealand the shift to a "demand-driven" student-choice model has shifted the onus of fee-setting to providers of tertiary education; the level of fees is one dimension in which institutions compete for students. Many OECD countries also have differential fees for some groups of overseas students. The basic advantages of differentiation is to augment total fees, and make institutions more sensitive to fee paying consumers while allowing them to charge fees which are related to their particular cost structures.

- *Shifting support mechanisms* from a system of non means-tested grants to a mix of means tested grants, more generous scholarships and income-contingent loans (loans based on the ability to pay principle; actual repayments depend on the post-graduation income of the borrower). These financing arrangements take the financial pressure off students while in higher education.

81

Of course it can be argued that poorer countries will find it difficult to match the US in terms of the availability and generosity of scholarships available to poorer students. Not only is the US more affluent, but there is a tradition of philanthropic giving to higher education which may be lacking in other countries. In the US scholarships have enabled poor but able students relatively easy access even to the most expensive universities. Almost half of Harvard students and 40% of those at Princeton, Yale and Stanford receive financial aid. On average such assistance amounts to a 40-50% discount on student costs. It will be difficult for other OECD countries to match these figures from private sources. Endowments, charities and employers can be asked to contribute more, and over time they may be expected to do so. But the unconstrained ability to set fees also contributes to the ability of these elite institutions to offer generous assistance to poorer students; increased fees themselves increase the scope for redistribution.

Income contingent loans can be thought of as a mechanism for currently drawing on some of the future private returns (*i.e.* borrowing against future earnings), repaying only when and if they can afford to. Of course there are many details which need to be considered. Should loans and repayments be administered by private sector financial institutions or via the tax system? Should students be able to borrow only to cover fees or should they be permitted to borrow for maintenance as well? Should interest be paid, and if so at what level (UK loans only require repayment of the principle in real terms)? New Zealand is one OECD country that now has a genuine income-contingent loans scheme by which students can finance not only tuition but maintenance, although means-tested student allowances to cover living costs are available for low-income students.

One transitional problem for countries switching to a loans system is that there are considerable up-front costs; it takes time for repayments to accumulate and the system to reach long-term break-even (or whatever long-term target has been set). One possibility for generating an immediate injection of resources would be to sell outstanding public sector student loans to the private sector (securitise the loans). Selling these outstanding debts to the private sector each year generates ongoing government savings.

The argument for requiring students to bear a higher proportion of the costs rests on the substantial financial benefits they receive from tertiary education. In spite of some serious technical problems associated with pinning down these benefits accurately (how much of the higher earnings of graduates are due to tertiary education and how much to intrinsic ability, family background factors, etc.?), few doubt the gains are substantial. For example, relative to earnings of those with upper secondary education only, the earnings of women aged 30-44 are 24 and 61% higher for women with non-university tertiary and university tertiary education respectively. The corresponding earnings gains for men are 18% and 57% (OECD, 1999). Comparing private costs and benefits to estimate rates of return, a very wide range of studies exists showing high private rates of return both absolutely (in excess of 10%) and relative to alternative investments available to individuals. On equity grounds there is no justification for subsiding these high returns to individuals from relatively privileged backgrounds out of general taxation. These subsidies represent, on average, redistribution from low to high-income households. This is not to deny that there may be sub-groups within the tertiary education population for which the returns are low or for which the subsidy is genuinely redistributive. Furthermore, as the tertiary population grows, it seems likely that at the margin it will be necessary to attract young people from less privileged backgrounds. On equity grounds it will be important to monitor reforms of tertiary financing to ensure that they do not create access problems for such groups. This point is taken up again shortly.

The arguments for state financing should, in principle, depend on market failure and equity arguments (although, as in other areas of public expenditure, history and tradition have probably been as important in determining actual financing modes). However, these arguments have not been particularly well made. In particular, the externality arguments claiming that higher education confers on society in general a layer of additional returns over and above those captured by graduates, have usually been asserted rather than proved. Another body of literature relates higher education to overall economic growth, see for example Temple (1999). Paradoxically, where externality and public goods arguments are perhaps most plausible, in the area of university research, private funding has grown most rapidly. This is partly due to governments making their own research funding contingent on raising private finance. Nevertheless, it is likely that for a combination of such reasons society does benefit from higher education over and above private returns, but there are no sufficiently reliable or robust estimates on which the optimal financing contribution out of general taxation could be determined. The fact remains that the bulk of the benefits are captured by individuals. They could, therefore, be asked to bear a greater share of the costs.

The suggestion that greater cost sharing in tertiary education is likely to form part of the financing strategy for lifelong learning reflects trends that are already observable in many OECD countries. Thus, between 1995 and 1998 nearly one half of OECD countries reported an increase in private spending on tertiary education institutions of more than 20%. In over half the countries for which the comparison can be made the private share of funding has increased, very substantially so for some countries (notably Italy and Hungary). It should be noted, however, that an increase in the private share does not mean that public spending on tertiary education has decreased. In all but three of the countries for which the comparison can be made, public spending has in fact increased. There is some evidence that countries with the highest growth in private spending also have the largest increases in public spending; the two sources of funds are complementary.[8]

The crucial question is whether reforms of the type suggested, even where the repayment of loans is income contingent, would deter enrolment, particularly the enrolment of children from disadvantaged backgrounds. Advocates argue that this should not happen because a) there will not be increases in up front expenses, as these will be covered by loans and scholarships, and b) because loan repayments are income contingent – repayments should never become burdensome relative to income. Furthermore, the inequality of access in many countries under current funding arrangements suggests that factors other than costs are at work in deterring participation by children from disadvantaged backgrounds in tertiary education. Nevertheless, the effect on participation can really only be determined empirically. Surprising little research exists which carefully examines the effects on participation in tertiary education of changes in the full direct and indirect costs actually borne by students.

Even in the US, which has by far the largest proportion of the age group in tertiary education, and one of the most effective systems for providing financial support for able students from low-income backgrounds, participation in college education, as in other countries, is strongly correlated with family income. If financial constraints are not the major factor in determining the pattern of participation in tertiary education in the US, the explanation must be sought elsewhere. Family and environmental factors are a strong candidate. Of course, environmental factors and borrowing constraints may *both* affect tertiary participation, but where family and environment provide the necessary preparation for successful tertiary education, simply relaxing the financial constraint by grants or subsidised loans to students from low income families may not be particularly effective. Helping families to provide the environment conducive to earlier development of scholastic aptitude would be more effective. Some evidence suggests that by the age of about 14 scholastic ability is largely determined, although malleable at earlier ages. The importance of family and environmental factors in determining educational success has of course been known for some time [Coleman *et al.* (1966) highlighted their importance, relative to school expenditure, in determining successful compulsory schooling]. A recent empirical test using US data is contained in Cameron and Heckman (1998).[9] They argue that scholastic ability, for which they have a test score measure, is the product of family and environmental factors, both of which are themselves in part determined by family income. They then estimate the effects of different factors affecting the probability of attending college. On its own, family income plays a big contributing role. But when pre-college scholastic ability is included as an extra explanatory factor, the importance of family income is drastically reduced.

They conclude from this that family and environmental factors, as embodied in the scholastic achievement score, are the driving forces in explaining college attendance. If short-term credit constraints were binding, then the effects of family income would not be so drastically diminished simply by including scholastic ability as an extra explanatory factor. In terms of policy, the implication is that interventions later in life, subsidising college for poor students for example, will be far less effective in promoting wider access to tertiary education than policies that intervene at much younger ages. The focus of such policy should be on building up scholastic ability, motivation and attitudes that predispose individuals to attend further education. This is not to say that financial constraints never matter. For some individuals in some countries they undoubtedly do. However, at the margin it will often be the case that more cost-effective means exist for improving access to tertiary education.

Of course, one needs to enquire further why it is that prospective students to US higher education are not resource-constrained and whether the same would hold in other countries if they reformed tertiary financing in the direction of greater cost sharing. Evidence that family and environmental factors play a major part in participation decisions can take a number of forms. At a general level the US experience is constructive. Yet, it can be argued that factors unique to the US explain why financial constraints are rarely binding on the participation decision. This is firstly because the existence of open access to two-year community colleges provides relatively cheap access to further education both in terms of opportunity costs and in terms of direct costs such as tuition fees and accommodation (many students in such colleges live at home). For students wishing to attend the elite four-year universities generous loan and aid programmes exist which are targeted at children from less affluent backgrounds. Further factors reducing the financial barriers to higher education participation in the US include the modular system which makes it easy to take breaks in study and to transfer, if need be, to cheaper institutions and a plentiful supply of part-time employment. Where such institutional factors are absent, shifting a greater share of the costs of higher education to students or their families could discourage participation more than it would appear to in the US. To put it another way, there is a strong case for accompanying funding reform with institutional reform designed to increase the range of institutions and qualifications on offer. The Austrian *Fachhochschulen* (established in early 1990s to offer shorter more vocational courses than universities) is but one example. The classical research-based universities will, of course, survive, but there is a growing realisation that the "one size fits all" model is not appropriate. Furthermore, institutional diversification may reduce costs per student in the sector, if only because some non-university tertiary institutions have shorter courses.

6. Public and private sector training programmes

a) *Empirical background*

The very diversity of types of job-related training for adults makes it difficult to provide a clear picture of the provision in different countries (the problems here are similar to those of documenting ECEC provision). Given the variability in intensity and quality, participation figures serve as a first approximation only (Figure 19).

Figure 19. **Percentage of 25-64 year-olds participating in job-related[1] education and training, by age, 1994-95**

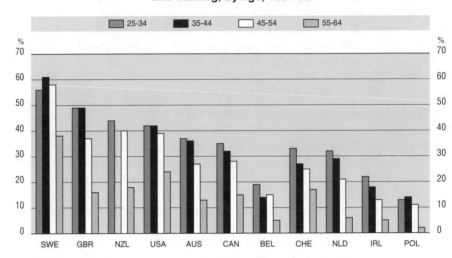

1. For Sweden, the percentages relate to all education and training, not just job-related.
Source: OECD (1998).

Not only are the country differences notable but, in general, the levels are quite low, given the wide definition of education and training. Only for Sweden does half the working aged population receive such training. For most of the OECD countries surveyed 60% or more of the workforce do not receive training. Except in Sweden and Belgium, men receive more training than women, but the discrepancies are not generally very large.

Figure 20 uses training expenditure as percentage of GDP to examine the public sector training "effort" across countries. The figure breaks down this expenditure (where possible) between adult training (for the employed and unemployed) and youth measures (training for unemployed and disadvantaged youth and support of apprenticeship and related forms of general youth training).

As in the enrolment measures, there is very substantial variation indeed across countries in the expenditure share of national income devoted to active training measures, and also in the emphasis given to youth versus adult training. This certainly suggests that this component of lifelong learning is one where low provision countries need to review their commitment.

Figure 21 documents the well-known tendency for those with more formal education to receive more job training as well. Except in Sweden, fewer than 30%

Figure 20. **Public expenditure as a percentage of GDP on labour market training, 1999[1]**

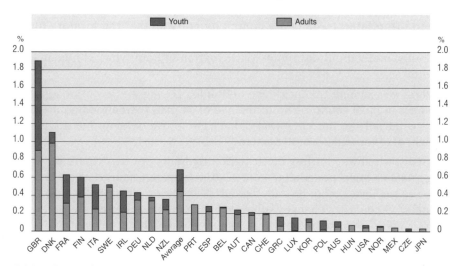

1. Belgium, France, Korea, Poland, Portugal, Switzerland, United Kingdom: 1998. Greece, Luxembourg: 1997. Ireland: 1996.
Source: OECD (2000).

Figure 21. **Percentage of 25-64 year-olds participating in education and job-related[1] training, by education level, 1994-95**

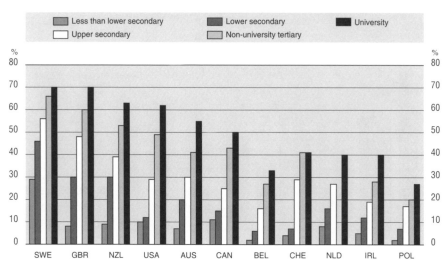

1. For Sweden, percentages relate to all education and training, not just job-related.
Source: OECD (1998).

of those with less than upper secondary schooling participate in training. In every country the increase in participation at successively higher levels of formal education is marked. There are (at least) two possible explanations; either formal education and job-related training are complementary so that the former enhances returns to, and hence participation in, the latter, or some unobserved characteristics (ability, motivation) determine participation in both types of human capital formation.

When we examine the incidence of training by age we do not observe great differences in most countries up to the age of 44, but, thereafter, training falls off rapidly, especially for the 55-64 year-old age group. We defer further discussion of the plight of older workers until Section 7.

Finally, when we multiply participation by hours per participant we find the average training hours per adult (Figure 22). Unfortunately hours data are lacking for Sweden so we have a more restricted group of countries. Nevertheless, we see that the ranking of countries changes somewhat (Canada does better, the Netherlands worse). It would also seem that these annual training hours are quite low, but to assert this meaningfully we would need some yardstick for adequate training, which we do not have.

Figure 22. **Mean numbers of hours per adult[1] of job-related education and training, 1994-95**

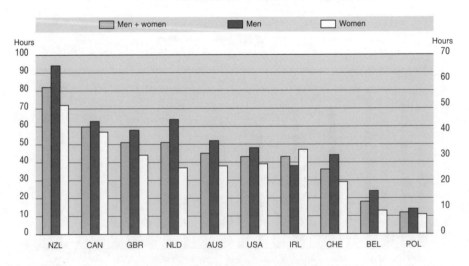

1. Mean number of hours per participant multiplied by participation rate, ages 25-64.
Source: OECD (1998).

b) Evaluation: what works in public sector training?

There is, of course, an enormous literature on the effectiveness of individual job training programmes.[10] In addition to monitoring the effects of specific interventions, this literature has sought to advance the science of programme evaluation.[11] Evaluation is difficult for some of the same reasons raised in the discussion of ECEC. For small demonstration programmes we do not know how to extrapolate results to larger populations or differently targeted populations. Even where programmes are successful, we rarely have sufficient variation in the data to know what components of the programmes (*e.g.* the classroom or on-the-job components) generated this success; vital information for designing more effective training as part of a lifelong learning strategy. This is not the place to review this literature in depth, but rather to attempt a very brief summary of what we know and to ask whether this knowledge suggests whether job training is a likely candidate for forming a central plank of a lifelong learning programme. It is difficult to generalise about the effectiveness of training because:

- Results vary across types of programme and across countries (much of the evaluation relates to the US and Canada, although European countries are starting to do more effective evaluation than in the past).

- Results vary across sub-groups of participants in training programmes.

- Results vary by evaluation criteria. Usually evaluation looks at the post-training earnings and employment records of participants. So far there has been little evaluation of the types of social outcome (reduced criminal activity, for example) that we showed to be important in ECEC evaluation.

- Estimating deadweight, displacement and substitution is intrinsically difficult.

Nevertheless we can say something. It is crucial to distinguish between private sector and public sector training programmes. The literature suggests the former are more effective, with rates of return clustering in the 10%-20% range, while very few public sector training programmes produce rates of return approaching 10% (Heckman, 1999), a possible exception being the US Job Corps programme. Of course, one is not really comparing like with like when comparing private and public training. There is a selection bias at work. Private sector trainees are more likely to benefit because they have been selected by employers or are self-selected. They are typically higher skilled to begin with than trainees in public programmes. Because of complementarities between types and levels of human capital, it will be the case, on average, that even within the group of employees the more skilled will attract and undertake more training. Both the training (because firms are better attuned to market requirements and changing skill demands than government agencies) and the trainees are often higher quality in the private sector. It is not generally profitable for private firms to make major efforts in training low skilled and disadvantaged adult workers.

89

For these reasons training and retraining of these more vulnerable groups tends to be left to public sector training programmes. Of course, there is much heterogeneity of outcome depending on the particular target groups (adult men, adult women, youth, displaced older workers) and on the nature of the actual programme. As a generalisation, one gets what one pays for; cheap and short programmes will have low or negative returns while more intensive, and expensive, programmes will have better results. Overall, however, the weight of the evidence suggests that such programmes have only modest, and not always permanent, impacts on earnings, employment probability, poverty and other programme goals. The group most likely to gain from public sector training programmes is adult women; adult men on average profit less, while the results for youth training are almost universally disappointing. Where different programme characteristics can be independently evaluated, it appears that strong links with local employers and a major on-the-job component are associated with success.

Due to the sheer heterogeneity of existing provision and the difficulty of formulating precisely what adequate, let alone optimal, provision would look like, adult learning and training is probably the most difficult sector to analyse and for which to make clear recommendations. Yet, this is precisely the area that most people have in mind when they think about lifelong learning. While job-related training is poorly funded by the state (relative to formal education and ECEC) it is far from clear what the appropriate role for public funding should be. The reality is that the state has assumed responsibility, by default, for the learning needs of those that private employers are unwilling to finance: the unemployed, the poorly educated and, in some cases, the older workforce.

In Chapter 3, we considered the incidence of on-the-job training costs borne by employer and employee, showing how the standard Beckarian analysis required modification in the light of market failures. It is difficult to know whether current levels of on-the-job training are adequate. The poaching argument suggests that they may not be in the absence of a training levy. Many governments allow both trainees and trainers involved in enterprise-based training to deduct expenses from taxable income; presumably this reflects a belief that the volume of such training would be inadequate in the absence of such subsidies. In Sweden, for example, the state subsidises enterprise-based training where the need arises due to restructuring, or where there is a perceived labour market need over and above the requirements of firms giving the training. As we know that the more educated and better paid receive disproportionate amounts of on-the-job training, we can say that these subsidies are not equity-promoting.

On-the-job training, however, is not the only aspect of lifelong learning for adults. Two other major components are adult general education and job training for the unemployed. Little formal analysis or empirical evaluation exists about how and how much the state should contribute to the finance and provision of the former, while empirical analysis of training programmes for the unemployed produces very mixed results as discussed above. In general, both adult education and training programmes for the unemployed are funded publicly (usually by local government or a combination of local and central governments rather than by central government on its own) although, especially where adult education is leisure or life-style oriented, a fee element enables some cost sharing. As a generalisation it is probably true to say that adult education has achieved relatively low priority from governments and its funding has been more vulnerable to economic conditions than has been that for compulsory schooling and post-compulsory secondary and tertiary education. Adult education has been particularly vulnerable when governments have needed to reign in public spending. Our analysis of the effects of technical change, sectoral demand and employment shifts and adult illiteracy suggests that lifelong learning strategies should re-examine the low priority currently afforded to this sector.

7. Older workers

a) *Empirical background*

Figures 23 and 24 show that employment rates for both men and women fall dramatically after the "prime-age" employment years (25-54).[12] In only a handful of countries are more than 70% of men or 60% of women over 55 in work. Of course, the age band 55-64 is a wide one, and a finer age breakdown would reveal a more gradual decline in the probability of employment with age. Nevertheless, it is remarkable, and not widely appreciated, that countries like Germany, Italy and France have less than half of their male population (and less than 30% of their female population) aged 55 and over in work. There are other implications, which we discuss shortly, but in terms of the now familiar discussions of the impact of ageing populations, these low employment ratios contribute to high dependency ratios, increasing the financing burdens of income support and health care for older persons.

The above relates to the current position (as far as data permit). In terms of changes over time both employment rates and labour force participation rates for older men have fallen dramatically over the last twenty years. While it is true that men of *all* ages are now less likely to be in work than they used to be, the reductions have been greatest for older men.

For women, employment rates have tended to *increase* overall, but older women have not benefited from this, their employment rates have remained largely unchanged. Table 12 illustrates both these trends for Britain.

Figure 25 shows that the downward trend in male labour force participation was quite widespread in the OECD for the twenty years up to the mid-1990s.

Figure 23. **Employment/population ratios by age, 1998**
Men

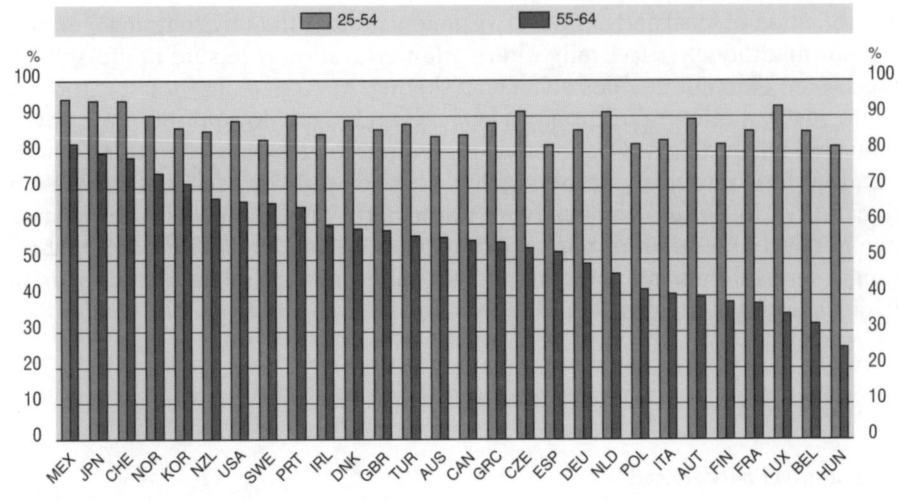

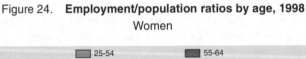

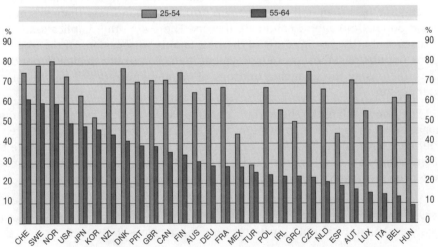

Source: OECD (1999*a*).

Figure 24. **Employment/population ratios by age, 1998**
Women

Source: OECD (1999*a*).

Table 12. **Employment and labour force participation rates (%),
United Kingdom, 1979 and 1997**

	Men		Women	
	All	Aged 55-65	All	Aged 55-60
Employment				
1979	90.8	79.4	60.2	50.9
1997	80.6	58.3	68.9	50.4
Labour force participation				
1979	95.1	83.2	64.0	53.1
1997	86.7	62.9	72.8	52.6

Note: The figures exclude students, under 18s and persons over state pension age.
Source: Campbell (1999).

The countries are ranked left to right in terms of the size of the percentage decrease, the Netherlands experiencing a massive 43% decline in male participation over the decade and only Japan immune from the trend of falling participation of older men.

Figure 25. **Male labour force participation, men aged 55-64, 1974-94**

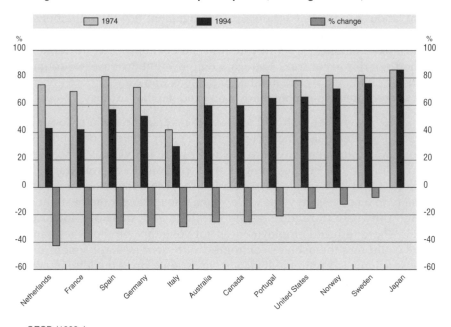

Source: OECD (1999a).

There is suggestive but not definitive evidence that the downward trend in male employment may have ceased in some countries (see OECD *Employment Outlook*, various issues); generally it has certainly slowed down. However, there is no current evidence of it being reversed.

b) Policy and lifelong learning implications

Does the decline in employment of older people matter? If so, what is the role for policy and, in particular, what role can lifelong learning play? It is sometimes argued that early retirement is an efficient mechanism for labour reallocation by replacing time serving older workers whose skills are becoming obsolete with more energetic younger workers with up-to-date skills. Leaving aside the question of how much truth this caricature of young and old workers contains, economies which already have high dependency ratios for purely demographic reasons can ill-afford the additional burden imposed by the foregone output of such a large proportion of the potential labour force. In public finance terms, the counterpart to this lost output is the reduction in tax revenue compared to the revenue with higher employment. Where early retirement leads to subsequent old age poverty, the public finances may also deteriorate due to increases in income support commitments.

It seems highly probable that there are lower cost methods of encouraging efficient labour allocation. Furthermore, the argument that the retirement of older workers makes room for younger more productive workers implicitly assumes that there is a fixed amount of employment in the economy. Except perhaps in the very short run this is not true. Aggregate employment increases over time and is ultimately determined by the number of persons who can compete effectively for jobs; if workers are employable there is no fixed number of jobs.

Whether governments should attempt to reverse the trend to lower employment rates for older males and increase the rates for women[13] depends in part on whether low employment rates are desired by the individuals concerned. Have the reductions in the employment of older persons been voluntary? If so, we could accept that individuals have decided that the benefits of early retirement (the ability to enjoy leisure years while young enough to get the best out of them) outweigh the costs (foregone labour earnings and, possibly, lower pension income). Where reduced employment is not voluntary, on the other hand, older persons could find themselves confronted with poor re-employment prospects and unexpectedly low retirement income. In extreme cases the latter may take the form of social exclusion and/or old-age poverty. Evidence that older workers at the lower end of the earnings distribution have a higher probability of being displaced would suggest that much early retirement is not voluntary.[14] Of course, in practice it is often difficult to know whether early retirement is voluntary. For example, a person may lose his or her job because that job is no longer needed in their employer's firm. This is clearly involuntary. That person may subsequently reject job offers and or drop out of the labour force because the wage they can command is substantially lower than in the previous job. This second stage is voluntary retirement but the underlying cause is involuntary job loss. Some recent evidence in Britain found that nearly two thirds of men over 50 who retired early did so under compulsion from their employers.[15]

To better evaluate the significance of falling employment rates for older workers, we need to examine in more detail the reasons for this trend. One of these could be an increase in labour market discrimination against older workers. Indeed, older workers often claim to feel marginalised at work and in job search. Empirically, however, it is difficult to establish the extent let alone the trend in pure discrimination. To do so one would have to show that workers who are alike in all relevant aspects except age have different labour market outcomes. The problem is that age tends to be correlated with other relevant characteristics such as amounts and quality of education and training, experience, etc.

So, leaving discrimination aside, there are two classes of explanation for recent declines in employment of older persons: skill-biased technical progress (SBTP) and the potential incentives to early retirement embodied in occupational and, to a lesser extent, state pension schemes. The general effects of SBTP were discussed in Chapter 2, but it is worth noting here that older workers are likely to be disproportionately affected. New skills are, not exclusively but to a large extent, introduced into the labour market in successive entry cohorts. By acting as a demand shock favouring younger skilled workers this puts older workers, even skilled older workers, into competition with young unskilled workers. This puts them at an even greater disadvantage than they would experience simply due to the long-term increase in the quantity and quality of education.[16] These effects of SBTP reduce firms' demands for older workers, increasing the layoff risk for the employed and reducing the re-employment probability for the unemployed. To the extent that lower employment rates of older workers reflect these consequences of SBTP, they do not reflect voluntary decisions.

It is difficult to generalise about the incentives to early retirement posed by pension schemes. To their holders, pension rights are capital assets. To the extent that the real value of these assets increases over time there will be a wealth effect. This will induce decreased hours of work, thereby encouraging early retirement. On the other hand, pension schemes where the pension income is related to final salary, added years of work tend to add disproportionately to the pension value,[17] constituting a disincentive to early retirement. Final salary schemes also discourage workers to move from full-time to part-time work. Such "downshifting" to a less-demanding job with the same employer can be encouraged if pension schemes are more flexible in permitting pensions to be calculated on a year, or

95

years, close to retirement rather than strictly on the final year of work. On the demand side final salary schemes create incentives for firms to create early retirement opportunities. In general, firms have incentives to either impose mandatory retirement to limit pension obligations, or offer early retirement schemes in order to reduce the workforce when faced with cost shocks. Where pension scheme provisions induce firms to encourage early retirement of their workers, the decisions are again not strictly voluntary. Under these circumstances workers may be dissatisfied with the level of retirement income they receive. In the past, state pension schemes in some countries also enabled early retirement, but generosity and eligibility have tended to become more limited as ageing populations increased the financing burden facing governments. Such tightening is likely to continue.

Governments should be careful not to encourage early retirement as a means of cutting labour supply, even in circumstances where they regard such cuts as desirable. It is expensive and in the long run could threaten the sustainability of social security programmes. There is clearly scope to reduce early retirement by changes in state and occupational pension rules. For example, many state pension schemes reduce the pension received when the pensioner has labour market earnings above some level. Reducing this implicit tax would create a substitution effect resulting in an increase in the desired hours of work of older workers. Increasing the deferral rate by which the value of the pension is increased if its take-up is deferred should have a similar effect provided the deferral is not actuarially unfair. In terms of occupational pensions in the private sector, policy would need to discourage firms from using such pension schemes as a relatively inexpensive way of retiring their workers early. One method would be to reduce the tax relief employees often receive on the lump sum component of their pension wealth. Another would be to raise the minimum age for occupational tax relief. Legislating against mandatory retirement would be another possibility, but its longer term effects on employment are far from clear.

Governments could simply subsidise firms to retain older workers, and indeed such subsidies may well form part of a package of measures designed to keep older workers in employment. Unfortunately, this approach is likely to incur large deadweight costs. Therefore, employment and/or wage subsidies should probably be used in conjunction with enhanced training and retraining to offset the effects of SBTP in shifting demand from older to younger workers. Public training of out of work men in general has low returns, and in the case of older workers they are likely to be even lower. A better approach is on-the-job training. Can such training simply be left to the private decisions of workers and firms? Probably not.[18] Private returns to training for an older trainee are low (see Box 2), primarily due to the relatively short period remaining to recoup the benefits, but also because opportunity costs (lost earnings during training) and risk aversion (uncertainty of returns to training) may be greater for older workers with family or other commitments.

Box 2.   **Effect on private returns of delaying human capital investments**

Wolter and Weber (1999) use data for Switzerland to simulate (based on a number of assumptions about costs and post-investment earnings) the returns to investing in different educational qualifications at age 40. They compare the returns firstly to having made the same investment at the earliest possible age and, secondly and more relevantly, relative to not having made the investment at all (*i.e.* relative to remaining, at age 40, at the next lowest qualification level). Delaying such investments reduces their return substantially (it is always better to train early) and makes the return to investment at age 40 either negligible or negative (it may not be worth training at all if delayed too long). For example, if males were to invest in university degrees (either vocational or "theoretical" in orientation) at age 40 the consequence would be a *reduction* in the present value of lifetime earnings. Acquiring a qualification from a higher technical college would increase lifetime earnings, but by an insignificant amount. For women, the effect of investing at age 40 is also to reduce lifetime income, except for those with no post-compulsory schooling who acquire the lowest level of vocational training.

So subsidies are likely to be required to induce firms to provide the relevant training. At the same time there may be some scope for firms to examine their career pay structures to see whether these currently discourage their workers from retraining. On the other hand, in reasonably competitive labour markets firms may have little room for manoeuvre; the need to pay higher wages would constitute a disincentive for firms to finance the training and/or to hire retrained workers. Public subsidies could make the returns to retraining higher for both workers and firms. Such subsidies would most usefully cover a proportion of the opportunity cost of training or retraining for older workers. Tax holidays on post-training earnings would be another method of increasing the private rate of return to training for older workers. Financial incentives aside, workers have to be convinced of the appropriateness of the training on offer. The precise nature of the retraining needs of older workers needs to be considered in detail in the context of individual countries. In general, it is worth remembering that retraining is not only to enable workers to stay with existing employers. Training in the use of computers and IT, for example, can facilitate the reallocation of older workers from declining-employment sectors to expanding sectors; from agriculture or manufacturing to services, for example.

We have argued that there may be strong equity grounds for subsidising retraining or other lifelong learning programmes for older workers and less skilled workers, who are vulnerable to the effects of technical change. However, it needs

97

to be realised that such subsidisation may be inefficient in rate of return terms; the available evidence points to low returns to human capital investments for these groups. We have seen that the highest rates of return are to be found in ECEC and small scale high quality programmes targeted to young people. Not only is there a longer payback period, but learning complementarities favour early investments and investments in more highly skilled workers. An efficient policy would be to invest in the learning of the young and the skilled, tax away some of the returns and use these to support the incomes, but not necessarily the jobs, of displaced older workers and unskilled workers. This argument is to some extent undermined if one assigns intrinsic value to employment. Indeed there may be strong reasons to do so; work confers dignity and prevents the growth of a dependency culture. The fact remains, however, that investing in these groups will have low economic returns, and the widespread use of wage or job subsidies can be both very expensive and involve serious inefficiency if employers dismiss existing workers in order to substitute workers who are eligible for subsidies.

All the above discussion of lifelong learning policy towards older persons has been in terms of retaining them in the labour market or inducing them to return where they have become economically inactive. It can also be argued that some lifelong learning resources should be directed towards older people simply to enhance their quality of life, irrespective of labour market implications. For example, given the Internet resources now available, policies aimed at improving the computer literacy of older people who are currently unable to access the Internet could considerably enhance the quality of life during retirement. For such non-labour market investments it is difficult to know, even in principle, what the appropriate level of public subsidy should be.

8. Strategies to raise benefits and/or reduce costs

Given that implementation of a lifelong learning strategy is likely to encounter resource constraints, it is imperative that money is spent as efficiently as possible on both existing and new learning modes. Innovative delivery can reap cost savings on existing education and training, releasing resources which are potentially available for expansion of lifelong learning. By the same token, given government budget constraints and competing demands for scarce public funds, proposed initiatives are most likely to be adopted where they can be shown to be cost-effective.

We have shown above that certain areas of educational spending appear *not* to be cost-effective; existing studies show them to have low net returns. Of course these past rates of return are only a guide to the efficiency of future spending if funds are used exactly the same way as in the past and if the environment in which future investments occur is very similar to the past. Both assumptions could be false. The recent increases in returns to tertiary education (particularly but not exclusively in the US and UK) provide an example where using past rates of return would have been inappropriate for investments whose returns will accrue in the future. So, faced with *ex post* low returns, policy-makers may react by looking for ways to improve the effectiveness of both existing expenditure and proposed increases in spending.

a) Improved certification and documentation

One aspect of reform is simply to improve information about courses and sources of finance to potential users. We turn to this shortly. But it may also be important to improve information about what students have achieved on different types of courses. Primarily, of course, this information is useful to potential employers and thus can increase the employability of course participants. Better documentation of what has been learned in education and training will also make it easier for individuals to pick and mix within an expanded lifelong learning framework. Certification and quality assurance is, of course, a vast topic; some of the basic issues are raised, but no pretence is made that what follows is a comprehensive discussion.

In essence, the question of reforms to qualifications and certification systems is relevant because if such reforms lead to greater agreement about what skills and competences result from individual components of lifelong learning there should be greater portability of skills between jobs and across learning modes. In turn, this will increase the potential benefits, and, *ceteris paribus*, the rates of return accruing to the individual lifelong learning components.

In many countries reform of qualifications and certification procedures has a double objective; to achieve parity of esteem between vocational and general education on the one hand and between work-based and education-based learning on the other. One route to this objective is to increase cross-sector recognition of qualifications within the formal education sector to facilitate credit accumulation and transfer across sectors. If pathways and credit exist – for example from vocational to academic education or from two-year to four-year tertiary institutions – there is less risk of certain types of education and training being branded as "second class". This should improve the willingness of learners to opt for the courses most appropriate to their preferences and abilities, rather than select inappropriate learning strategies on the basis of perceived status. Within formal education improved certification is likely to remain primarily the responsibility of national education authorities.

In Denmark, for example, recent reform of vocational education (VET) and training enables students to acquire qualifications for university entrance alongside their vocational qualifications. The reform also introduces the concept of a

99

"partial qualification" for students unable to complete the full VET qualification. Another innovation which increases the visibility of VET activities, both to education authorities and to prospective employers, is the "educational portfolio" or "log book". This documents an agreed personal education plan, the actual study sequences (including course regulations and requirements) and the learning outcomes (College examination documents), a description of the qualifications and competences achieved by the student during the overall learning process both in educational institutions and the workplace. Where appropriate a copy of the apprenticeship agreement is also included. Austria has also been providing double qualification pathways in its full-time schools.

Much more difficult is to provide credit for the diverse range of courses and non-formal learning and training that are available after the years of formal education. Non-recognition of such learning acts as a disincentive to learners. It could also distort choices by driving individuals into inappropriate types of learning simply in order to get a more widely recognised qualification. Where countries do make serious efforts to increase the transparency and portability of qualifications, and to enable returning adults to enrol in formal education on the basis of what they know rather than on the basis of their highest previous qualification, incentives for both individuals and firms to invest in adult learning could be increased. Assessing and certifying workplace skills and competence will involve greater co-operation between national governments and the private sector than required in the case of quality assurance in formal education. One should not, however, underestimate the difficulties of achieving comparability and recognition for the very diverse learning modes that exist outside the formal education system.

b) Harnessing new information and communication technologies

Potentially, one of the major channels for ensuring cost-effectiveness is by exploiting the productivity of new technologies. However, it is important not to get carried away. Futurologists talk glibly and hopefully of a world in which the new information and communication technologies provide education on an "anyone, any time, any place" basis, utilising the likes of two-way, voice-activated, computer-assisted learning. Reliable figures are difficult to come by, in part because there is not as yet any standardised treatment of ICT in school accounting systems, nor even a standardised definition of what to include in ICT expenditure.[19] It is clear, however, that universal (or even widespread) adoption of such state of the art technology lies far in the future. Nevertheless, evidence suggests that expenditure on ICT in primary and secondary schools is increasing faster than other categories of educational spending and educational spending as a whole. In the US spending on ICT has outstripped spending on books and other printed material. However, this growth is from a low base and, even in the most ICT-advanced countries in the OECD, total ICT spending accounts for only between 1 and 2% of the total expenditure for primary and secondary schools. These figures probably understate educational usage of ICT and its growth, because much of the action may be in professional and business access and/or home usage. In spite of the rapid growth of ICT expenditure, there still remains a lack of high quality learning materials designed for on-line delivery and a lack of software that facilitates the use of such materials. At all levels the reality for many remains "chalk and talk" with teachers teaching to standard curricula in large classes and many poorly motivated pupils. Resistance to change can of course be self-motivated, but it can also be argued that the personal contact required in older teaching technologies is a vital component of effective and fulfilling education.

Other unanswered questions relate to the effects on quality and standards; both students and employers need to be convinced that distance learning utilising ICT does not represent a dilution of quality. Quality assurance mechanisms and mechanisms for recognition and accreditation of qualifications from technology-based distance learning are in their infancy and will require international co-ordination and co-operation. Furthermore, with technology changing rapidly it is difficult to foresee its use in education reaching a steady state equilibrium in the near future. However, the real cost savings of the new technologies will only be reaped in some kind of steady state, or beyond some threshold at which the high set-up costs of introducing new learning modes are spread across large numbers of students. It is also necessary that newly introduced technology can be used for a number of years before major replacement or major revision. If the technology deemed pedagogically appropriate is constantly changing, planning technical change in education becomes exceedingly difficult, and cost savings are difficult to achieve as updating or changing technology incurs substantial "switching costs" for both suppliers and users. More prosaically, even acknowledging the potential of new technologies to reduce costs, there remain a host of resource allocation decisions that can only be taken "on the ground". What is an appropriate (cost-minimising) mix of old and new technologies? Within the ICT budget in schools and institutions of higher education, what is the appropriate split between hardware, software, content development, technical support and teacher training? There will not be unique answers to such questions. Efficient utilisation will depend on the level of education, the capabilities of students and teachers, the subject and a host of other factors including relative factor prices, which differ from country to country. Nevertheless, at a more general level, and in the context of lifelong learning, use of new information technologies can, in principle:

- Improve the quantity and quality of information available to both the suppliers and demanders of lifelong learning.

- Reduce unit costs in learning delivery.

- Increase access to learning opportunities.

In the annex to this chapter some specific examples of the use of new technologies that contribute to these aims are described.

At a more micro level than the initiatives described in the annex, new technology can be used to alter the teaching technology of existing courses or specific learning objectives within existing educational institutions. To reduce costs, utilisation of ICT would involve capital-capital substitution as ICT replaces some existing equipment and textbooks as well as the substitution of capital for labour. Currently, little research exists on a systematic basis estimating the cost savings achievable using this approach. It is not to be supposed that the process of such substitution is costless; even where savings are achievable over the longer run there will be, at this disaggregated level as at an institutional level, substantial set-up costs if the new technologies are to be effective. Educators and technicians will need to co-operate in course design and delivery. The initial costs of such developmental activities can be high.

If little evidence is available on potential cost savings, the picture is not a lot clearer with regard to the pedagogical effectiveness of the use of new technologies, although some piecemeal evidence exists. A US study (Wenglinsky, 1998) showed that while computer aided instruction can affect mathematics scores of eighth graders, the impact depended more on *how* teachers used computers (simulations and applications were more effective than drill and practice) than on the intensity of computer usage.

Instead of teachers using computers in the classroom, another approach is to use the multimedia or the World Wide Web as an instructional tool. A *priori* there are many advantages; flexibility of timing and scheduling, direct access to a wide variety of international resources, a less threatening learning environment than with some face-to-face learning situations, user-paced and self-directed learning.

Lockyer *et al.* (1999) report on a controlled experiment in which undergraduate students on a module in an Australian Bachelor of Physical and Health Education degree programme were randomly assigned to traditional and Web-based learning. The two approaches were evaluated both on specific learning (knowledge) outcomes and learners perceptions of effectiveness. Learning was shown to be significantly more effective in the Web-based environment than in the classroom and, in addition, the vast majority of learners perceived the Web-based environment to be as effective or more effective than face-to-face classroom learning.

Financing partnerships in educational ICT

Due largely, but not exclusively, to the technical complexity of ICT delivery and usage, a multiplicity of alliances already exists. To describe these as public-private partnerships is not incorrect, but disguises the complexity of the arrangements involved. Governments, educational institutions, libraries, software firms and hardware suppliers, publishers, radio and TV stations, telecommunications companies all co-operate in various permutations to supply a complex and differentiated market. OECD (1999) describes an initiative between Intel, Hewlett Packard and Microsoft to train teachers on the effective integration of technology into existing classroom curricula. The same source also provides examples of OECD countries where governments have negotiated discounts with telecommunications companies for Internet Access, installation of telephone lines and classroom wiring.

c) *Administrative reforms*

Where existing arrangements are unduly fragmented and uncoordinated, resulting in waste of resources due to duplication and inconsistent policy, cost-effectiveness can be increased rather simply by administrative reform. In the UK plans exist to reform non-university tertiary education to meet some aims of life-long learning. The government is setting up a Learning and Skills Council with an annual budget in excess of £6bn (much greater than university sector budget). The council will take over and co-ordinate the function of the existing TECs (Training and Enterprise Councils) and the Further Education Funding Council as well as taking responsibility for regulating and funding sixth formers in schools. The objective of establishing this new body is partly to oversee an expansion of the sector. The aim is to enrol another 600 000 in next two years (on top of current stock of about 4 million). More generally, however, the new council is seen as being needed to improve the cost-effectiveness of further education and training. This will be achieved, it is envisaged, by having the central council setting the parameters of regulation and funding but with a series of local councils planning actual provision in partnership with colleges, schools, businesses and local authorities.

Initial reactions to the proposal have been favourable, particularly from the Colleges of Further Education which are often perceived as being second class in relation to sixth forms and private training companies funded by TECs.

Notes

1. Unless otherwise stated, the source is OECD (1998).

2. The Perry Project took place in Michigan in the 1960s. Other intensively studied model programmes in the US include the Carolina Abecedarian Project conducted in North Carolina from 1972-1985.

3. The evaluation issues discussed in relation to the Perry programme raise a more general problem encountered when applying existing evaluations to lifelong learning strategy. Most such evaluations refer to relatively small programmes with non-representative target groups. Typically, such evaluations examine the effect of the programme in question without considering effects of the programme on the "non-treated" population; they use a partial as opposed to general equilibrium methodology. But some components, at least, of a lifelong learning strategy will have wider effects, and these can render unreliable evaluations using partial equilibrium methods. Suppose, for example, it was decided as part of a lifelong learning strategy to subsidise the costs of tertiary education. If this subsidy led to large enrolment increases one might expect that, *ceteris paribus*, graduate earnings would fall and non-graduate earnings increase, due to relative supply effects. In such a case, existing rates of return based on the assumption of fixed relative earnings would overestimate the effects of the subsidy. In another context we would expect that any large scale training subsidies would have significant displacement effects and deadweight (see below) so that evaluations based on the earnings gains of trainees may overestimate social returns unless these general equilibrium effects are taken into account.

4. See US National Research Council (2001) and Ontario Children's Secretariat (1999) for further information and references on early brain and child development.

5. For further discussion and evidence relating to quality dimensions of ECEC see US National Research Council (2001) and references in Currie (2001).

6. Yet another indicator of tertiary coverage is the proportion of school leavers graduating to tertiary programmes. On average four out of ten school leavers are likely to attend tertiary programmes leading to the equivalent of a Bachelors degree, although in some countries (the Nordic countries, Poland, Hungary, New Zealand) the proportion is better than one in two (OECD, 2001).

7. This argument is couched in terms of institutions of higher education delivering approximately the same mix of outputs as currently. Of course if the mix were to change, say by introducing a range of shorter courses or a higher proportion of teaching-only institutions, one could not assert so confidently that sustained reductions in real per capita funding would eventually lead to reductions in the quality of output.

8. The figures quoted in this paragraph are from OECD (2001).

9. Cameron and Taber (2000) also fail to find evidence of binding borrowing constraints in US schooling choices.

10. An alternative approach seeks to relate the effectiveness of job training programmes and other active labour market policies to macroeconomic indicators such as the unemployment rate, see for example Nickell (1997).

11. Some important contributions include Lynch (1992, 1994), Lalonde (1995), Heckman, Lalonde and Smith (1999), OECD (1999), the latter two references containing comparative information on rates of return to training.

12. A similar pattern is observed for activity rates (labour force participation rates) and much of the argument in this section applies to these as well as to employment rates. Because older unemployed workers are less likely to find employment than younger workers (they experience longer unemployment durations), it can be argued that employment rates better capture the true labour market status of older workers. Furthermore, *changes* in employment over time have generally been reflected in inactivity rather than unemployment.

13. Female employment rates may be expected to increase somewhat with the ageing of cohorts of married women with higher employment rates.

14. See Campbell (1999) for such evidence relating to Britain.

15. Sarah Hogg, "Longevity means early retirement cannot work", *The Independent*, 2 May 2000.

16. In addition, current cohorts of older workers experience labour market disadvantage due to the ageing baby boom increasing their relative supply.

17. For illustrations relating to Britain see Disney and Whitehouse (1996).

18. However if, as seems likely in the lifelong learning context, there is a general trend for more frequent retraining, older workers should benefit from this to some extent.

19. OECD (2001) provides some recent estimates. For example, in 1999 the percentage of primary school pupils using computers ranged from 25% in Italy to over 90% in Canada, Finland and New Zealand.

Annex to Chapter 4

The Use of New Technologies to Deliver more Cost-effective Lifelong Learning

The annex provides some specific examples that have been used or have been proposed as means of improving the quantity and quality of both learning and information about learning opportunities, of *reducing unit costs in learning delivery and increasing access to learning opportunities*. A characteristic of many of these examples is their "clearing house" or "brokerage" nature. Courses and learning materials are bought in rather than produced in house. In some cases the function is simply to bring together users and providers.

Learndirect (UK)

Learndirect aims, primarily, to provide impartial information and advice on courses and finance which will enable adults (over 18) to plan and implement learning appropriate to career development. Thus, individuals who have been out of the workforce for some time, those wanting to change career direction, those needing to retrain due to recent or imminent redundancy can all benefit from information relating to local career advice, the local availability of courses, financial support, childcare facilities, etc. Employers can also benefit by receiving advice on appropriate training for their employees. Special arrangements are available to people with special needs. It is operated in conjunction with the Ufi (see below); the free Learndirect helpline being seen as an integral part of the Ufi, providing information on Ufi-approved courses. Although there will be local Ufi learning centres where individuals can meet Ufi advisors, Learndirect will be the first entry port to the Ufi for many users.

Distance education

Distance education is a major growth area in educational provision. Although it comes in many shapes and sizes, a common characteristic of distance education is that learning normally occurs in a different place from teaching. There are usually two central components to distance learning: independent study of course materials and interaction with other course participants (tutors, other students, technicians). Although new technologies are revolutionising both components, they probably have the greatest effect on the interactive component. Interaction can be asynchronous where participants are not required to be present simultaneously (email, computer conferencing) or synchronous where interaction is in real time (audio and video conferencing).

The potential cost advantages of distance education and other information systems based on new ICT technologies depend crucially on the scale of operation. Modern information industries, of which distance education is an example, tend to share a common characteristic: information is costly to produce and cheap to reproduce. Once the "first copy" has been produced the cost of distributing the information using new technologies is very low.

Furthermore, the variable costs tend not to increase even if a great many copies are made; there are no obvious capacity constraints to increase incremental costs, as say labour shortages can do in non-information industries and also in conventional modes of delivering education. In other words, with high fixed costs and low variable costs, economies of scale are particularly important in distance education. While fixed costs (*e.g.* capital expenditure, course development and testing, all of which are independent of number of users) are higher than with conventional educational institutions, the variable costs (transmission and other costs that *do* vary with student or user numbers) are lower. Distance education reaps a cost advantage when it can spread its fixed costs over a sufficiently large number of students so that total (fixed plus variable) unit costs are lower than in a conventional institution. Marginal costs – the costs of expanding or contracting the number of users at the margin – will always tend to be lower for distance learning as these costs are independent of fixed costs.

Of course distance education is far from new. There are a number of well established examples of the use of ICT to provide distance learning. The UK's Open University (OU) is a case in point. Currently over 200 000 students study OU courses, and since its establishment in 1969, it has provided higher education for more than two million people. Both the age range and educational and socio-economic backgrounds of students are more heterogeneous than is the case in conventional universities. It has been estimated that the cost per student at the OU is about one third of that at conventional universities and the cost per graduate about one half. Other OECD countries have followed suit. For example, Japan and Korea now also have their well established tertiary distance learning, catering both to "conventional" tertiary students and offering additional lifelong learning opportunities for disadvantaged adults. The Japanese University of the Air was established in 1985 and now has a student population of approximately 62 000, while the Korean National Open University (KNOU) enrols over 200 000 students and is the largest single provider of higher education in Korea.

Technical change has opened up new forms of distance learning; today there is less reliance on correspondence learning and greater emphasis on computer-based learning, interactive video, video conferencing, and utilisation of satellite networks. Here we highlight some more novel examples, most of which share the characteristic of not, for the most part, developing their own learning materials but brokering, franchising and repackaging existing materials and using new delivery technologies to provide wider access to these existing materials.

The UK University for Industry

The Ufi is intended as a new kind of organisation for open and distance learning. It is intended to be fully operational by 2004. The government forecasts that by 2002 some two and half million individuals and businesses will be using the Ufi's information services, with perhaps 600 000 per year actually pursuing its learning programmes. The strategic objectives of the Ufi are to:

- Stimulate demand for lifelong learning among businesses and individuals by providing a clear route to learning opportunities.

- Promote the availability of, and promote access to, innovative learning opportunities through the use of ICT.

It is envisaged that these objectives will be met by stimulating new markets for learning, by improving the quality of learning resources and reducing the costs of accessing the learning.

Utilisation of the latest information and communications technology is central to the conception. Some examples are:

- On-line access to enquiry, information and registration systems.
- Websites and bulletin boards giving direct access to providers.
- Provision of technical and personal support to individuals using multimedia technology.
- Links with tutors and other students via Ufi e-mail.
- Refinement and improvement of learning programmes by customer feedback.

The very high set-up costs of providing quality distance learning are avoided, because rather than deliver its own learning material or award its own qualifications it will mainly broker high quality products from other organisations. The Ufi is an *enabler* and *broker*, helping to identify and achieve learning targets for individuals and firms. Such products will be made widely accessible at times and locations (home, workplace, approved learning centres) to suit the users. Broad partnerships (education providers, employers, trade unions, voluntary groups) of public and private institutions will attempt to identify skill gaps, trends in employment, attitudes towards learning, and the quality of existing learning programmes. Where there are perceived gaps in provision it may commission multi-media learning or information products to fill these gaps:

- Basic literacy and numeracy skills.
- ICT skills for the workplace.
- Business management skills, for small and medium sized firms.
- Initial efforts will focus on four sectors where there are existing and/or forecast skill shortages (automotive component production, multimedia, environmental technology, distributive and retail trades).

As with distance educational provision in general, the costs of Ufi/Learndirect will depend crucially on the scale achieved. Fixed costs will be high, but once up and running supplying information to additional users will be cheap (Box 3).

The Swedish Forestry Project Initiative

In Sweden, a more limited project is located in the forestry industry. The Forestry Project Initiative provides out of working hours distance learning, computer based learning and interactive video facilities to provide shift workers in the industry with core upper secondary education, because the industry has difficulty in recruiting personnel with the three years of upper secondary education required to manage the highly computerised and automated technology in pulp and paper processing. The project is partially government financed but employers are responsible for providing suitably equipped ICT learning centres close to their factories and for paying supervisors in these centres.

The African Virtual University

A non-OECD example of innovative distance learning is the African Virtual University (AVU), currently in its advanced pilot stage. Serving sub-Saharan Africa the AVU uses interactive satellite and computer-based technologies to train scientists, technicians, engineers, health care providers and other professional workers. As in the case of the e-university and the Ufi, the AVU mainly buys in courses, library facilities and laboratory demonstrations from existing high quality educational institutions (to date from the US, Canada and Ireland). Problems of declining budgets, outdated and scarce building and equipment, inadequate

Box 3. **Small business and the Ufi – the UK vision**

Many small – and not so small businesses – have told Ufi that their needs involve training. These include: how to improve financial management, how to market effectively, the best methods to recruit good staff, how best to manage a team, and how to cope with regulatory requirements efficiently.

To address these needs and make learning and training more accessible, the Ufi is designing bite-size modules that address very specific business needs. These modules can be worked through at a convenient time and place, whether at work, home or, perhaps, a local learning centre. Regardless of which module and learning location is chosen, the courses will be of the highest quality and at the right price.

Under the brand name Learndirect, Ufi is introducing a new approach to training. Using the best features of on-line delivery a growing range of highly targeted learning products will be provided.

Ufi will offer taster courses through the Learndirect website to enable customers to check the quality and appropriateness of courses before they are purchased. Being available in bite-sized chunks the Learndirect courses enable users to fit training requirements in line with their business's pressures and lifestyle.

The initial Learndirect portfolio of courses for managers of smaller firms includes:

- Recruitment and selection
- Understanding finance
- Winning more business (selling and marketing effectively)
- When to coach
- Your coaching style
- How to coach
- Practical coaching situations
- Using cash flows to manage
- Managing working capital
- Understanding working capital
- Appraisal interviewing
- Facilitation skills
- Mentoring skills
- Equal opportunities
- The effective leader
- Team building
- Coaching skills
- Reviewing a coaching experience

109

supplies of high quality faculty are all especially acute in parts of Africa. Nevertheless, the AVU as an example of the use of technology to overcome such constraints, and to enable wider access to high quality tertiary education, is of broader significance.

The Norwegian Network and Information Technology Project

The establishment of new institutions such as the Ufi and the AVU is not the only way of harnessing the new ICT to improve learning cost-effectiveness. New technologies can be utilised within single or groups of existing institutions. One example is the Norwegian Network and Information Technology Project (NITOL). Box 4 reproduces a description of this initiative from OECD (2000*a*).

Box 4. The Norwegian Network and Information Technology

All Norwegian universities and colleges are connected through an electronic infrastructure. Some universities and colleges are now co-operating to offer students on and off campus electronic access to lessons given in these institutions via the Internet. By combining the use of relatively inexpensive equipment such as video cameras and computers in the classroom, student off campus have access to lessons simultaneously with students on campus. This allows for flexible access to tuition both by students and teachers – the student can access a lesson when it suits his/her timetable and the teacher can integrate the lessons of others into her/his own courses. The institutions currently participating in this project have agreed a contract for co-operation, including the sharing of learning materials. In addition, electronic conferences are set up for communication between teachers, students and tutors, so that seminars, discussion groups and the setting and marking of assignments can be carried out in a more flexible and cost-effective manner. In a two-week period, for example, tutors taking part in this project were able to answer 2 000 questions from 570 students. To date approximately 2 000 students have participated in this type of open and flexible learning environment each semester. This autumn, about 90 different courses will be offered in open and flexible learning mode. These courses cost on average about one fifth of more conventional courses, depending on the amount of preparation, guidance and follow-up work required, and are thus considered very cost-effective.

UK e-university

Another example is the proposed *e-university* (the electronic university) in the UK. Although many details are still to be worked out, the basic idea is that students will sign for degrees awarded by existing institutions. These universities will market electronic versions of their own courses (or bought in and re-branded courses). Although under the wing of the Higher Education Funding Council and expected to receive at least £50m pump-priming from government, the e-university will be run as a partnership with one or more private companies providing hardware and software and taking a stake. Furthermore, the e-university is expected to be autonomous and able to set its own fees. Initially, the e-university will offer vocational and quasi vocational courses such as engineering, technology, business, law, medicine, computing, and economics, although once established a wider menu should be feasible. Although in the UK a primary aim will be to attract overseas students and earn foreign exchange, exploiting what is felt to be an area where the UK has a clear comparative advantage; there will also be many domestic adults wishing to update skills or change career. In principle this will be a way of broadening access to tertiary education by reducing costs and offering education on a more flexible basis than is possible under conventional teaching arrangements.

Chapter 5

Mechanisms for Financing Lifelong Learning

1. Introduction

Because of the wide range of activities encompassed by even fairly modest lifelong learning scenarios, and the size of the participation and expenditure gaps (see below) that would have to be closed in order to realise them, it is almost self-evident that:

- Full implementation of the lifelong learning concept will require additional resources; current education and training budgets are unlikely to stretch to the implementation of the kinds of lifelong learning strategies currently envisaged by Member countries.

- Some of these additional resources will have to come from governments; some net additions to public spending are likely. Realistically, however, with many OECD countries attempting to reduce the proportion of their GDP accounted for by public expenditure, such additional extra public funds will be limited. The case for raising additional funds for lifelong learning, either from net additions to public spending or by diverting funds from other expenditure categories (either within the education budget or from non-educational budgets), will have to be cogently argued.

- For the same reasons, it will be vital that maximum efforts are made to ensure that both existing and new public expenditure on lifelong learning are cost-effective. In fact, re-examination of existing programmes, both in formal educational institutions and in labour market programmes, may be necessary in order to explore the potential for cost-savings so as to release funds to previously neglected areas.

- Because the scope for potentially worthwhile lifelong learning initiatives is large, and the potential for financing them publicly is limited, the responsibility for implementing lifelong learning cannot rest with government alone. Incentives will have to be found which will mobilise resources other than from the public purse; financing from multiple sources – financing partnerships – are likely to be a vital component of implementing lifelong learning strategies.

Naturally, the discussion of financing mechanisms appropriate to specific countries cannot be considered separately from each country's lifelong learning goals, operational objectives and its time horizons for achieving these. Nor can the analysis ultimately ignore the specific economic and social context of lifelong learning policy formation. Some countries are currently further ahead[1] in providing lifelong learning opportunities than others. According to a synthesis of country reports submitted to the OECD (OECD, 2000a), the Scandinavian countries, Japan and the Netherlands are currently achieving at least adequate lifelong learning provision, the Czech Republic and Hungary have major shortfalls, while Austria is somewhere in between. For countries with relatively advanced provision, where all the basic elements are in place, the obvious priorities will be to constantly monitor and improve existing programmes. Such countries will typically place less emphasis on developing new financing partnerships to mobilise additional funds. On the other hand, countries with larger lifelong learning shortfalls face major challenges in simply establishing all the basic elements of a lifelong learning system. Typically, they will be less able to rely on modifications and extensions of existing funding schemes and may have to rely on more radical alternatives. This distinction should not be overstated, however. The countries with more comprehensive lifelong learning provision already in place are typically countries with above average tax burdens and may well come under increasing pressure in the future to contain or reduce taxes. Efficiency savings and the mobilisation of non-governmental lifelong learning funding will be advantageous to these countries also.

While we will refer further to country-specific approaches to lifelong learning and its funding as we proceed, they are not our primary focus. While fully acknowledging the importance of relating analysis and policy recommendations to the specific goals and prevailing conditions in individual countries, an in-depth consideration of such country-specific parameters could immerse us in a mass of detail. Our objective here is somewhat different. While alluding to country experience and strategies illustratively, we attempt, where possible, to consider general principles. These in turn should inform detailed policy-making and country-specific implementation.

Various administrative reforms, institutional innovations and financing mechanisms are considered, with particular emphasis on learning accounts and related schemes.

The focus is on some relatively new ideas and approaches to the financing of lifelong learning. Of course, not everything new is good or *vice versa*. However, this is not intended to imply that certain mechanisms that have been around for some time, such as training levies or granting favourable tax status to training expenditure by trainers and trainees, cannot have desirable effects.

2. Using existing resources more efficiently

The overwhelming importance of teachers' salaries in the costs of formal education prompts the question of whether, in the light of the failure of empirical research to establish unambiguous learning or earnings gains from smaller classes, higher pupil-teacher ratios could be safely used to increase cost-effectiveness in formal education, at least at the secondary school level. Indeed, some OECD countries, with large participation gaps to close (Hungary, the Czech Republic) have little alternative but to follow this route. In other countries (Norway, Japan), greater use of ICT has been used in part to substitute for teacher input. In general, however, cost savings from larger classes is a solution to be treated with some caution. Firstly, the evidence on class size effects is not unambiguous; some studies do report learning gains associated with smaller classes. Secondly, increasing class sizes would undoubtedly worsen conditions of employment for teachers and could lead to problems of recruitment, retention and increased pay pressure. Thirdly, whatever researchers find about their effects, large class sizes are unpopular with parents. This suggests that it would be politically difficult to use larger classes as a major source of cost cutting in formal education.

Even where class sizes are not substantially increased, savings on labour and capital costs can, in some cases, be achieved by *institutional mergers*. Where this has occurred (the Netherlands in the 1990s is a prime example) it has partly been in response to demographic trends; smaller school populations can justify rationalisation to release resources to other educational and training needs.

More fundamental reforms in financing and modes of provision may be appropriate in some cases:

- *Increasing competition*. Although several OECD countries have both public and private provision in the tertiary sector and in adult training, primary and secondary education are on the whole shielded from competition (Japan is one country that has used private providers in all sectors of education). One possible reform would be to challenge the local monopoly status enjoyed by many schools by introducing more competition into the compulsory schooling sector [see Hoxby (1999, 2000), for evidence of the performance enhancing effects of school competition in the US]. In the country reviews commissioned by the OECD several countries report moves to generate a limited market in education. While this could involve public and private institutions competing against each other, there are other means of encouraging competition. Essentially switching funding from institutions to students ("consumers"). Where consumers have the discretion to choose providers, *i.e.* where institutions are paid only for the students they enrol, institutions have a strong interest in demonstrating high product quality.[2]

- *Fiscal incentives.* Even in the absence of markets or pseudo markets it may be possible to provide institutions with incentives to increase cost-effectiveness by allowing them to retain the "profits" they make from any cost savings. The Danish "Taximeter" scheme (see Box 5) is an example.

- *Devolution of funding.* In some countries, where centrally raised funds are channelled through and administered by local government, head teachers and school governors complain that the bureaucracy involved not only absorbs resources that would be better used in the schools themselves but also discourages innovation and experimentation. The basic rationale here is that decision-makers closer to the operational realities will make more effective decisions. Where there is evidence in support of this argument, there may be a case for granting greater autonomy to school heads in how funds can be spent. Similar arguments for granting autonomy to school heads and governing bodies may apply even to funds raised by local taxation. Some central control is likely to be retained if for no other reason than the pursuit of equity goals; children's life chances should not be unduly influenced by the tax base and social goals of the area they happen to live in.

- *Output-based funding.* Some governments are now rethinking the way they allocate public funds in compulsory education (and, indeed, to other areas of government spending). Essentially, they are moving, or intend to move, away from input-based block grants [*i.e.* funding on a per pupil or per student basis (with other resources such as teacher salaries, etc., estimated on historical pupil-teacher ratios and average expenditure data)] towards output or performance based funding. Such a switch can, in principle, provide greater incentives for efficiency by requiring greater accountability and transparency in how institutions operate. Greater accountability and improved quality assurance in formal education institutions are either in place or under active consideration in many OECD countries. Nevertheless, output-based funding raises the perennial problem of output definition and quality measurement in educational institutions. If output is defined too narrowly, or if the weights to be given to multiple outputs (*e.g.* teaching and research in the case of universities) are not specified or are incorrectly specified from a social viewpoint, the system can become distortionary. Institutions concentrate on activities they know will be rewarded by current rules. For example

116

Box 5.   The Danish Taximeter Scheme

This funding scheme is designed to strengthen institutional incentives (mainly in tertiary education and adult training) to increase efficiency by cutting costs but not at the expense of quality.

The main features of the scheme

- The incentive to cut costs is provided by setting taximeter rates based on estimated costs per student (including imputed infrastructure costs) of completing particular programmes. If actual costs exceed these rates, no top ups are provided and cross subsidisation will be required from more efficient programmes in the institution concerned. On the other hand, if *ex post* costs can be held below the taximeter rate, institutions can retain the "efficiency bonus" to improve quality and/or develop new educational initiatives.
- Institutions cannot abuse the system (in the long run) by lowering the quality of provision in order to attract efficiency bonuses. Because the system is largely demand driven – students have freedom of choice in where they enrol – institutions will have to demonstrate quality provision to continue attracting them. If they cannot compete, they will fail to attract students and their funding will fall.

Some problems

Although the system is generally regarded as working well, it does contain some structural difficulties:

- Because taximeter payments are guaranteed to approved institutions on the basis of enrolments it makes required outlays unpredictable. In 1998 there were large enrolments in certain types of adult training, and the Ministry of Education was confronted with unexpectedly high expenditure commitments. Steps are being taken to enable large unforeseen fluctuations. These include setting up reserve funds to deal with unexpected funding requirements, quantitative enrolment limits and the freedom to vary student fees.
- How often should taximeter rates be adjusted? If the rates are not revised often enough system wide this is like a very short-lived patent; institutions cannot reap the full reward for making cost savings and the incentive to do so is again reduced.
- Institutions which rapidly increase enrolments can be confronted by severe short-term hardship. This is because in order to relate funding to output only a portion of the full taximeter payment is paid for enrolling students, the remainder being paid on graduation. Thus rapidly expanding institutions will not be receiving funding commensurate with the student population they have to teach.

they may "skim" the pool of applicants and enrol only those likely to meet programme objectives. Furthermore, the substantial resources consumed in these exercises have, to some extent at least, undermined the support they receive from personnel in the institutions being evaluated.

3. Partnerships

As a generalisation it is probably true to say that, world-wide, governments are seeking to become less involved in the direct provision of goods and services and adopting instead the role of facilitator and regulator. This will surely apply to new initiatives in lifelong learning. We would not expect to see governments involved as sole direct providers of lifelong learning or even taking sole responsibility for financing them. The British Private Finance Initiative (see Box 6) is an example of government involvement which stops far short of old-style public sector provision. Although not currently used for lifelong learning-type projects,[3] there is no intrinsic reason why it could not be. Implementing the lifelong learning vision, at least those components beyond primary and secondary schooling, will necessarily involve a wide spectrum of partners. Apart from governments, employers and individual learners, finance and delivery is likely to include quasi-public institutions, non-governmental organisations, not-for-profit organisations, charitable organisations, trades unions, etc. In developing such partnerships attention will need to be paid not only to the proportions of public and private finance, but also to how the private burden should itself be distributed. For training and retraining this becomes a question of what proportion of the costs should be borne by firms and by individuals.

In the light of the above arguments it seems a reasonable prediction that many lifelong learning initiatives will be financed by some version of the class of financing arrangements generically known as Public-Private Partnerships (PPPs). Many OECD countries have in place some versions of PPPs. The UK's Public Finance Initiative is an example. It is an open question in applied public finance as to how far the approach can be extended. Initially, PPPs have tended to be restricted to ancillary services supporting core government activities; contracting out catering, cleaning and maintenance in hospitals or schools is, for example, quite widespread. However, the possibility of extending the role of PPPs to delivering actual core services in health, teaching, running prisons, etc., is not only being actively discussed but the first steps have been taken.

In the context of lifelong learning we need to consider whether the guiding principles which can ensure such mechanisms are consistent with, or even promote, the goals of equity, accountability and efficiency.

Box 6. **The United Kingdom Private Finance Initiative**

The Private Finance Initiative (PFI), introduced by the Conservative Government in 1992, retained and expanded by the ensuing Labour governments, is a public-private partnership mechanism that seeks improved value for money relative to pure public sector provision. By December 1999, agreements for over 250 Private Finance Initiative projects had been signed by central and local government for procurement of services across a wide range of sectors, including roads, rail, hospitals, prisons, office accommodation and IT systems. These projects range in capital value from less than a million pounds to several billions of pounds, and have an aggregate capital value of approximately £16 billion. Following the election of June 2000 all indications were that PFI-type funding of public services would be substantially extended in Labour's second term.

PFI differs from both privatisation, on the one hand, and from contracting out, on the other. It is not privatisation because the public sector retains a substantial role either as enabler or purchaser of the services provided. Nor is it simply contracting out because the private sector under PFI is typically a provider of the capital asset as well as a supplier of services. The general aim is to bring the private sector more directly into the provision of public service with the public sector as acting as enabler and procurer of services and as a regulator. There are several types of PFI project. At one extreme are financially free-standing projects where the private sector undertakes the project on the basis that costs will be recovered entirely through charges for services to the final (usually private sector) user. At the other extreme are projects where services are sold to the public sector, the cost of the project being met wholly or mainly by charges from the private sector provider to the public sector body which let the contract. A range of joint venture projects lie between these extremes. One important distinction is between schemes in which the asset is or is not transferred from the private sector supplier to the public sector customer at the end of the project. In virtually all cases the private sector supplier has responsibility for designing, financing, constructing, managing and operating the project.

Why should PFI provide better value for money? At one level the rationale is a simple specialisation/division of labour argument. The private sector specialises in the provision of goods and services and the bearing of risk. Furthermore, it is generally perceived to employ superior management techniques. Of course, to realise these potential advantages, PFI contracts must be put to competitive tender and they must embody appropriate incentives to private efficiency. They do so in part because payment to the private sector contractor only begins when a satisfactory flow of services is provided (making delays and cost overruns unattractive to private contractors) and subsequent payments depend on meeting performance criteria (providing an incentive to ensure efficient design of the capital asset). Further incentives are provided by the close integration of service needs with design and construction, because both are the responsibility of the service provider. In general, specifying the contracts in terms of outputs is seen as essential to achieving value for money.

Box 6. **The United Kingdom Private Finance Initiative** (*cont.*)

What the public sector specialises in under PFI is establishing the framework of policies and the legislation within which the private sector operates, deciding on which services should be provided from public funds, and clearly defining the contract requirements and, finally, procuring these services and managing the contracts.

One aspect of specialisation according to comparative advantage, which is central to PFI, is risk allocation; there must be a transfer of risk to the private sector supplier. In PFI contracts, therefore, there is not normally any guarantee or indemnity payable by the public to the private sector to cushion the supplier against cost overruns or unexpectedly low levels of demand or other forms of project failure. Exceptions may arise where it can be shown that such failure is a consequence of government action, but the latter excludes general tax and legislation changes, unless these have a major and discriminatory effect on the project. Residual asset value risk (how much will the asset be worth when the contract terminates?) and technology and obsolescence risks may be less clear cut and negotiated on a project by project basis. One risk generally retained by the public sector is that of wrongly specified service requirements. Even here, however when requirements cannot be fully specified at the outset – as in some ICT projects – there may be scope for risk sharing.

How successful has PFI been? There have been criticisms of major administrative inefficiencies and of failure of some PFI contracts to deliver the benefits promised. Shortcomings have been demonstrated most visibly in the IT sector where there have been a number of high profile problems in delivering against the original specification. Nevertheless an independent report commissioned by the UK Treasury reviewed 29 PFI projects (about a third of those PFI projects that were operational at the time of the research) and concluded: "The average percentage estimated saving for our sample of projects against the PSC (public sector comparator) was 17%. On the basis of the public sector's own figures, the PFI therefore appears to offer excellent value for money" (UK Treasury, 2000).

Partnerships are often contentious. Some have claimed that PPPs will only deliver small efficiency savings, if any. Others argue that a new "partnership sector" could transform the delivery and quality of public services. To date there simply is not sufficient long-term experience with such partnerships to be able to deliver a definitive verdict. In the meantime it would be unrealistic to think of PPPs as a panacea, either with respect to delivery or funding. This is not to say that we must await further evidence before extending the partnership approach; where the objectives are sufficiently pressing and the constraints on pure public financing are binding, judicious experimentation can be justified.

The idea of a public private partnership can cover a number of possible arrangements:

- The PFI version in which the private sector designs, finances, builds and then either operates or maintains the underlying asset. Ownership of the asset may revert to the public sector at the end of contract.

- Joint ventures.

- Profit sharing arrangements.

- Long-term contracts.

Nevertheless, before any particular partnership model is adopted and entered into, three questions need to be addressed:[4]

- Why and how the partnership can be expected to generate higher levels of total investment in lifelong learning?

- Why and how it will lead to quality improvements in service provision?

- Why and how it will result in better value for money?

The use of PPPs inevitably involves formal contracts between the parties. The skill and foresight brought to bear in writing such contracts is likely to be a central factor in determining the success or failure of PPP initiatives. One common element of virtually all PPPs is that they embody a degree of risk sharing/risk transfer. A central element in delivery contracts, therefore, must be a clear statement of which elements of risk are being transferred to the private sector and which are retained in public sector. Another vital aspect of such contracts is to make them sufficiently flexible so as not to lock parties into outdated outputs or delivery modes, etc.

Another cross-cutting issue that has attracted much attention relates to transferral of staff; what is the appropriate regulatory framework to govern the terms and conditions of staff who move across sectors? Career development, training, etc. One benefit of PPP growth could be a freeing up of the barriers between public and private sector employment more generally. Because PPPs are project-based they must address challenges which transcend narrow government departmental focus. PPPs may in themselves be a spur to the adoption of a more holistic approach to project design and evaluation.

4. Innovative financing strategies: individual learning accounts and related mechanisms

This section examines some innovative funding strategies under discussion or in operation (in some cases on a trial basis) in OECD countries. One difficulty in drawing conclusions from this analysis relates precisely to the newness of the initiatives; they have so far been subject to little empirical evaluation. Where possible we do look at what research has been done, but often this is very little. This is work in progress.

A general principle for maximising the cost-effectiveness of innovative strategies is to avoid excessively piecemeal reform by exploiting the underlying complementarities between them. This entails planning and developing interrelated reforms in parallel. A concrete example of this principle is the mutually reinforcing nature of financial and learning innovations. Financial innovations such as individual learning accounts could founder if holders have inadequate information about eligible courses and programmes, just as the latter will only be taken up if the financial incentives are in place. Thus, to take an example from the UK, holders of ILAs may be offered a year's free membership of the University for Industry, and information about this linkage could be highlighted on the Learning Direct helpline (see annex to Chapter 4).

Individual learning accounts (ILAs) are one of a number of novel financing mechanisms currently being piloted and researched in some Member countries (*e.g.* the UK, Sweden) as a means of putting flesh on the bones of the lifelong learning vision. ILAs belong to a general class of policies aimed at providing incentives for individuals to increase their asset holding. Before describing, and where possible evaluating, some specific proposals, a brief outline of the rationale for such policies is provided. At the same level of generality some cautionary notes are sounded.

ILAs belong to a class of policy initiatives aimed at extending asset building (or "stakeholding") to sections of the population which do not generally participate in such activities. Asset-based policy, with its emphasis on savings and investment, may be contrasted with many traditional welfare policies that tend to emphasise income and consumption.

Although ILAs and related initiatives are relatively recent policy innovations, the idea of asset-building incentives is not in itself a new one. The two most common forms of asset holding that are officially encouraged, generally via the tax system, are home ownership and saving for retirement. However, such policies as tax relief on mortgage interest payments and on contributions to retirement pension accounts often favour the better off. The poor tend not to own houses or have retirement accounts; where they do their marginal tax rates are too low for tax-based policies to yield substantial benefits. Initial discussions of ILAs and individual development accounts (IDAs) have focussed on their effects on poorer households.

It can be argued that income support and subsidising asset accumulation are complementary policies; supporters of asset-building approach do not call for abolition of income support. In fact it is important for the two sides to be considered simultaneously to avoid them working against each other. One obvious way in which this could happen would be where the asset testing of welfare payments acts as a saving disincentive to holders of government sponsored accounts. There may also be scope for reallocation of some funds from the income-consumption to savings-investment domains. For example, many OECD countries spend large sums on allowances to families with children, often not even means-tested. One possibility would be to transfer some or all of these allowances to children's savings accounts.

Some degree of complementarity notwithstanding, the choice between subsidising wealth rather than income cannot, in general, be avoided. If one is to argue for subsidising asset accumulation rather than supporting income one could do so:

- Because of the particular nature of capital market imperfections.

- Because asset-holding changes behaviour in ways more beneficial to individuals than does income support.

- Because reducing wealth inequality should take precedence over reducing income inequality.

In a world where perfect capital markets enable individuals to smooth consumption over time by building up and running down assets, there would be no essential difference between subsidising income and capital.

In real world capital markets imperfections are likely to abound. Do such imperfections suggest that governments should be encouraging asset accumulation? Suppose that market imperfections imposed greater impediments to borrowing than to saving. In such circumstances poorer households would be better served by income support. There is no doubt that some households, especially low-income households, can face punitive borrowing rates, supporting the need for income subsidies, at least for purposes of consumption smoothing. On the other hand low-income households are often non-taxpayers and therefore do no benefit from tax incentives to saving. Limitations on the level of assets that can be held while preserving eligibility to certain types of welfare payments are also a disincentive to savings. As implied above, this is only an argument in favour of asset building subsidies if these assets are "forgiven" when calculating benefit eligibility.

An often-cited capital market imperfection is the difficulty of borrowing against future expected income. This makes financing education by borrowing from financial institutions impossible or expensive. (This is one reason why many student-loan schemes have heavy government involvement.) Assisting individuals to build up sufficient savings to finance human capital investments could help to offset such borrowing constraints. However, it is not clear that purely in terms of overcoming borrowing constraints, ILAs and similar policies are superior to alternative methods of support such as subsidised loans or even outright grants.

The most common rationale for encouraging asset holding is that it influences individual behaviour in socially desirable ways. Thus advocates have argued that

123|

such policies can have beneficial effects on saving, entrepreneurship, health, educational participation and attainment.

While such effects are not implausible, it is difficult to be certain about causality. Evidence on the savings rates or forward planning or educational participation of holders of ILAs or IDAs is not in itself sufficient. Individuals with strong motivation to save, plan or participate in education may self-select themselves into such programmes. We cannot be sure that the programmes have altered behaviour unless we have particularly rich panel data or data from randomised experiments. Nevertheless, programmes which include incentives for regular saving and which include an element of financial education, are more likely to affect behaviour. Of course making effective financial education a part of the programme increases its cost.

Naturally, one cannot simply *assume* beneficial behavioural effects. It is in the nature of such asset building schemes that the outcomes are uncertain. Why is this?

In terms of mobilising resources for lifelong learning, ILAs work by encouraging individuals and households to save more than they otherwise would and then encouraging savers to use these assets to fund leaning. The incentives provided by public subsidy will be largely judged against this objective. But suppose low income individuals or households are target savers – they aim to generate a certain stock of assets to fund learning, pay off the mortgage or just provide insurance against unforeseen circumstances. By increasing wealth, learning and development accounts enable these targets to be achieved by lower not higher savings out of current income. Furthermore, individuals may divert funds from other forms of asset holding to take advantage of the incentives attached to ILAs. Simply looking at the amounts held in ILAs does tell us their net effect on savings.

A similar problem arises on the expenditure side. ILA proposals generally embody restrictions on how the funds in the account can be spent; on approved education and training for example. But if individuals can substitute between spending from current income or alternative asset holdings it may be difficult to know whether spending on lifelong learning from ILA funds is a net increase in spending.

Presumably very large increases in the subsidy offered to account holders may be effective in generating net savings increases and net increases in learning outlays. However, not only does this increase the cost of the programme but it could itself generate adverse incentives, for example households may borrow in order to reinvest in learning accounts to avail themselves of the higher rates of return.

A more effective way of minimising such deadweight and substitution problems is by careful targeting. Savings subsidies should be directed to low income households with low savings and educational expenditure. However, targeting is itself not without its drawbacks; one may question the wisdom of encouraging very low income households to reduce already low levels of current consumption. Similarly, targeting those with low or non-existent expenditure on human capital may not be effective if the reasons for low expenditure are not merely financial constraints. Policy would need to address a wider range of reasons for low rates of return to learning expenditure for certain groups of individuals.

The implication of the above arguments is that governments introducing ILAs or related accounts will have to give careful consideration to setting a rather large number of parameters. These will determine the behavioural outcome for individuals and thus the overall net benefit of the policy. Among such parameters are:

- *The coverage of the scheme.* Many proposals such as the Swedish ILA scheme and the UK Child Trust Fund are intended to be universal, at least after initial pilots. Many of the US IDA programmes, on the other hand, restrict eligibility to low income groups.

- *Access to funds and permissible use of funds.* Subsidisation of asset-building usually requires, as a *quid pro quo*, that the asset is used on a range of investments likely to improve life chances; business start-ups, learning, home ownership, pensions and the like. However, it is feasible to allow a proportion of the asset to be spent without such restriction; this would be in keeping with the intention that subsidised asset-building should foster socially responsible behaviour, including spending decisions.

- *The level of subsidy.* Governments will have to decide on the extent of subsidy to build in to an ILA programme. The optimal subsidy will depend on how the objectives of the programme are defined (in terms of savings and learning outcomes for example) and the tightness of the government's budget constraint. In terms of the overall cost from public funds, there is likely to be a trade-off between coverage and generosity; more narrowly targeted schemes can afford a higher subsidy per account holder.

- *The instruments for delivering subsidy.* To the extent that ILA schemes are targeted to low-income households, the tax system is likely to be a relatively ineffective instrument. Many account holders pay little or no tax and are therefore unable to benefit from tax credits. For these reasons initial government contributions to the account and/or matching of subsequent contributions are likely to be the chosen instruments. On the expenditure side, subsidy can be delivered in the form of cost reductions on approved learning expenditure of account holders. Where it is desired that employers become effective partners by contributing to the ILAs of their employees, the arguments against using the tax system do no apply; here tax credits could be effective. They could reduce overall labour costs or, more specifically, the costs of training provided to employees. Similarly, tax incentives

125|

may be appropriate incentives where contributions to the accounts are sought from friends and relatives.

- *The timing of the subsidy.* Should whatever level of subsidy is agreed on be an initial one-off contribution or should it be spread over the life of the account, either in the form of subsequent fixed contributions or matching of account holders deposits over time? The argument for not giving the whole subsidy "up front" is that spreading the subsidy over time keeps the accounts "live" thereby encouraging and reinforcing regular saving.

- *Participation of account holders and co-contributors in investment decisions.* ILAs could, in principle, be linked to different investment strategies, embodying different degrees of risk and return. What role should account holders have in choosing the risk profile of their accounts? Involvement in such decisions is consistent with the financial education objective of asset-building strategies.

- *What level of private financial sector involvement is desirable and feasible.* While the UK experience (see below), is not encouraging, experience with IDAs in the US has managed to bring private sector institutions on board to a greater extent. While this could reflect an expectation that account holders would one day become profitable customers, in reality a stronger motive is likely to be that participation in such schemes can stand private financial institutions in good stead in relation to the extent and severity of government regulation of their overall activities.

ILAs and related schemes are still at a developmental stage, with many of the finer details to be finalised in countries proposing to introduce them. However, in spite of the need to firm up important details, the broad outlines of how ILA schemes might work are now clear. We discuss some examples.

a) The Swedish ILA proposal

The Swedish scheme is currently being piloted and refined. It is hoped to introduce accounts as of 1 January 2002. The long-term goal is that in a fully developed system of ILAs, all individuals would hold accounts. Although holdings in accounts are tax deductible, costs to the public purse are restricted because in the long run the majority of funds in ILAs become liable to tax (when they are used), and thus generate government revenues. Tax deferral rather than outright tax reduction is what the individual benefits from. Thus the costs to the public revenues in terms of lower tax revenues mainly occur in the initial build-up phase and diminish as the system approaches long run balance.

- The contributions to an individual's learning account, whether from the individual or employer, are subject to earned income tax relief for the account holder.

- Currently individuals can save up to SEK 18 300 (approx. US$2 100) per year. This sum is one half of the "base amount" – a unit used in planning ILAs in Sweden. The maximum amount that can be held in an account is ten base units. To prevent the ILAs being used simply to supplement pension savings, the right to invest further funds and gain tax relief ceases when the balance of the account reaches this amount. Of course, if the balance is reduced for spending on education or training further contributions can be made.

- Employers can contribute an additional half base amount on which the individual also receives tax relief; the employer's contributions are treated in the same way as the individual's when they have been credited to the account.

- When funds are withdrawn from the account they are treated as taxable income. In this sense the tax inducement to saving is a form of tax deferment rather than permanent tax reduction.

- However, funds used for approved learning ("competence development" in the terms of the Swedish proposal) attract an additional tax subsidy (a "competence grant premium"). A wide range of education, training, and work practice will be eligible. Currently the maximum reduction is SEK 9 150 (just over US$1 000).

- Two different versions of the competence grant premium are being contemplated:

  - A basic contribution from the government of SEK 2 500 (just under US$300) for all persons aged between 35 and 55 who, in year 2000, had a maximum annual income of SEK 180 000 (US$14 000) and who open an account in year 2002 and who contribute the same amount (as a minimum).

  - The second version directs the subsidy towards employers. They receive a one year reduction (figures between 5% and 10% have been suggested) of the payroll tax due on that part of an individual's salary contributed to his or her ILA.

- Funds in an ILA not used by the age of 65 are transformed into pension savings.

b)   ILAs in the UK

While initially resembling the Swedish scheme, the UK proposals as they now stand are much less far reaching.

- For one million starter accounts the government will contribute £150 for each individual in the first year of the account, subject to a small (£25) contribution from the individual.

- ILAs are accounts with government. There is no actual account in a financial institution, operated by a passbook or similar mechanism.

- Anyone (over 19 years old) can hold an ILA, but to attract a public contribution holders must be in the labour force, not in full-time education or on training schemes already publicly supported.

- Employees will not be liable for tax on employers' contributions to ILAs for eligible courses if contributions also go to low-paid workers.

- Employers can make tax-deductible contributions if used for agreed learning and if contributions also go to low-paid workers.

- ILA holders will receive discounts (20% standard) on eligible training courses (subject to a maximum expenditure on courses).

- Higher discounts (up to 80%) will be available to ILA holders enrolling on key courses such as computer literacy.

- These discounts will be provided at the point of payment for learning, the individual paying the balance of the cost of learning minus the government contribution.

- Applications for accounts, details on eligibility for discounts and arrangements for learning providers to receive their government contributions will be administered by a Customer Service Provider, which will also provide account holders with updated information about their accounts.

Three broad classes of incentives can be detected in the literature and in pilot schemes:

- Matching of individual savings contributions, usually by state, but possibly by employers, corporations, financial institutions or sponsors. A degree of matching is likely to be necessary if accounts are to reach effective size as the savings of target groups are likely to be constrained by low discretionary incomes.

- The tax treatment of interest earnings. Such earnings can be taxed at low rates or granted tax exemption, at least until such interest income is spent.

- Savings in such accounts can be excluded from the savings limits determining welfare eligibility.

A key element in the long-term evaluation of ILAs, as with other new sources of finance, is the extent to which they actually generate new learning investments. Deadweight and substitution, the twin bugbears of subsidisation schemes, must be considered. Will the tax subsidies and learning discounts be claimed largely by those who, anyway, would have invested adequately in their own learning and training (deadweight)? Will individuals shift funds from existing asset holdings to ILAs to take advantage of the higher rate of return (substitution)? Will firms seek tax relief via ILAs by substituting ILA approved learning/courses for their own in-house training? As argued above, governments can attempt to counter the dead-weight problem by targeting publicity (and, possibly, eligibility for discounts as well) on groups with low human capital and those least likely to invest to augment their human capital. In practice, this will mean targeting the low paid, the poorly qualified, employees in small firms, and individuals who have taken a career break and now wish to return to the labour market.

In order to ensure maximum take-up it is important that the scheme is admin-istratively simple and not beset with excessive regulation (thus, there should be maxi-mum flexibility about how funds can be used, the timing and size of withdrawals, etc.). More difficult to achieve, perhaps, is ensuring that the returns to an individ-ual placing funds in an ILA are competitive with alternative uses of such funds. Where private sector financial institutions are involved in administering ILAs they too must have the right incentives. It is true that holders of learning accounts consti-tute a potential expansion of the client base for financial institutions. However, if account holders are, indeed, predominantly low paid and poorly qualified, this ben-efit could easily be outweighed if the administration costs of ILAs are large relative to the rather small amounts that such accounts would typically hold.

The experience of ILAs in the UK has highlighted some of these difficulties of establishing effective partnerships to finance lifelong learning. While ILAs are now "accounts with government" which operate like a membership scheme, member-ship granting access to the educational discounts on offer, they were initially designed as actual accounts operated through financial institutions, but with the parameters being determined by government. Thus, in 1995 two pilot schemes were operated (in Gloucestershire and Somerset) in which account holders opened Skill Accounts with the Midland Bank (now HSBC). The accounts were off the shelf savings accounts, with all normal banking rules applying (including the right of the bank to refuse an application). Holders had to commit to regular pay-ments through a standing order, the rationale being that this would encourage sav-ing and commitment to human capital investments. The saving element is currently absent from the UK model, although it could, in principle, be reintro-duced. Of the 3 000 accounts opened in Gloucestershire as of 1999 just under 50% were still actively saving. However, due to the change in the learning account framework under the new Labour government, the Gloucestershire accounts will be transferred to the national scheme. Whether the model could be made to oper-ate successfully thus cannot be known on the basis of this pilot. Certainly, future partnerships with commercial banks will have to pay close attention to how ILAs can be made profitable for private sector institutions. They will need to be con-vinced of two things: firstly that administrative and operating costs are not exces-sive in relation to the size of the accounts and, secondly, that the government's target groups will eventually become profitable customers in their own right. By the nature of the ILA scheme, account holders are likely to be drawn from individuals at the lower end of the earnings distribution (the Gloucestershire pilot confirmed this, although a small number of individuals with higher earnings opened accounts). For this reason financial institutions are, in essence, gambling that account holders will become more profitable clients as a result of the scheme (or because the scheme attracts individuals who are motivated to succeed).

There is a wider lesson to be drawn from this experience. The potential benefit of effective partnerships, particularly with private sector institutions, is to move financing away from pure public sector subsidisation to more broadly based resource mobilisation. On the other hand, effective collaboration with private sector institutions is difficult to achieve. Such institutions are not the makers or instruments of social policy. To participate in joint ventures with government the incentives have to be right. Prior to the ILA experience, the UK government failed to persuade the commercial banks to administer its student loan scheme for essentially similar reasons – the costs were too high relative to the perceived benefits. In the case of ILAs there had been earlier consultation and joint development efforts, as well as a greater recognition on the part of government that financial institutions required appropriate incentives. That this greater awareness failed to secure effective co-operation does not imply that effective public-private partnership in financing lifelong learning is impossible, but it does highlight some of the intrinsic difficulties of establishing productive partnerships.

Further grounds for caution arise when one looks at the history of educational voucher schemes which share some generic similarities with ILA proposals; both involve an element of government subsidy to be spent by recipients on approved educational services. The benefits claimed by voucher advocates, in particular the virtues of free choice and the expected dynamic supply-side response, are not dissimilar to the hoped-for benefits of ILAs. And yet for all the high-powered advocates of voucher schemes, and the numerous pilots and experiments, as far as the author is aware, no democratic government anywhere in the world operates a fully-fledged voucher scheme.[5] The reasons for this are many and complex, one of which is the potential for fraud in any funding mechanism that separates payment from consumption (ILA schemes usually propose that to claim the subsidy, payment for a course is made to the learning provider rather than the account holder). Even in tightly controlled and minutely observed voucher pilot schemes educational institutions were found to exaggerate enrolments to claim government money for fictitious pupils. Of course, ILAs differ from educational vouchers in a number of important respects. So some of the disadvantages of the latter may be avoidable; nevertheless vouchers are a prime example of an educational funding reform that generated enormous interest but, to date, have failed to deliver. If ILAs are not to be another still-born initiative their advocates may profit from studying the history of voucher proposals.

c) **The Child Trust Fund proposal in the UK**

Perhaps the most ambitious asset building proposal to date is that of the UK Labour Party which intends to introduce a universal account, opened for all children at birth with an endowment paid in by the government. Known officially as the Child Trust Fund proposal (but unofficially as the Baby Bond proposal!) many details are yet to be determined.[6] Current thinking is that the scheme would be made progressive by having the initial endowment vary by family income. Other possible features include:

- The government endowment may be paid at key stages rather than as a lump sum at birth. One pattern is an initial payment at birth and subsequent instalments at ages 5, 11 and 16. As with the initial contribution, subsequent instalments may again be on a progressive basis depending on family income at the time of each instalment. Staggered payments help to keep the account "live" by reminding children and their parents that the funds are there and growing.

- Additional contributions will be permitted by parents, relatives or friends. Not only does this increase the value of the assets in the child's account but may stimulate household savings. Whether such additional contributions will attract tax credits is a possibility under discussion.

- Access to the fund will probably be restricted until the child reaches a certain age. An age of about 17 or 18 may be appropriate if funds are to be used to finance learning opportunities. Further restrictions may be placed on the use of the funds. Furthermore it may be desirable for parents or others making supplementary contributions to have access to these on a more permissive basis.

The UK government is also considering supplementing the Child Trust Fund with targeted adult accounts (the Saving Gateway) similar to US IDAs to encourage saving by adult groups who currently save little and have low wealth. Again, details are scarce, but it would appear that only households with low income would be eligible to hold such accounts. Incentives to save would be provided by the government matching (at some rate, and up to some maximum) the account holder's contribution.

d) **Individual development accounts in the US**

Unlike the Swedish and UK ILA initiatives, IDAs in the US (similar schemes also exist in Canada) have been in operation for some time and, for this reason, we have somewhat more evidence and evaluation of their effectiveness. For a description of some of the heterogeneous IDA schemes in operation by the latter half of the 1990s see Edwards (1997).

IDAs are matched savings accounts designed to enable low and moderate income households (although in principle the IDAs could be offered to higher income households; lower subsidy levels would operate) to build assets. Funds in IDAs can be used for funding education and training, starting small business, home ownership, etc. (depending on state legislation). Twenty-six US states have them, and there are in the neighbourhood of 300 community IDA programmes in operation. Their emergence has been primarily, but not exclusively, a local or state-based phenomenon.

The basic idea is very flexible as evidenced by large number of variations across US states:

- One such is a system of Individual Tuition Accounts to which employers, not employees, contribute. These are administered by the Council on Adult and Experimental Learning (CAEL) which has a membership of over 700 colleges, universities, corporations, labour unions and individuals. CAEL works with employers on education and training strategies, sets up the accounts and then advises employees on educational and training needs and opportunities on a one-to-one basis. In the mid-1990s there were approximately 10 500 such accounts held by individuals across the US with an average account balance of US$1 000 per year. The optimal size of an individual's account should be between US$2 500 and US$3 000 according to CAEL.

- Another is to allow seniors to open IDA accounts for their grandchildren's education (New Jersey IDA Demonstration).

- Some IDAs allow the matching rate to vary by family size in recognition of the fact that, for a given household, income is harder to save when there are larger number of dependants.

Table 13 cites some examples of operational IDAs in the US.

Evaluation of IDA *programmes*

Given the paucity of IDA schemes actually up and running, the evaluation literature is scarce. Some US results are examined shortly. However, a few general points can be made first. Obviously such schemes need to be evaluated against their objectives. These will differ for different asset building schemes, as will the weight accorded to particular objectives. Nevertheless, all schemes would appear to share the objectives of improving the distribution of capital assets, and of encouraging individuals to take more responsibility for their personal security and development. The latter is usually specified in terms of encouraging the savings habit and increasing expenditure in particular areas, learning being the relevant one in the current context.

Table 13. **Some illustrative examples of IDA programmes**

State	Programme	Eligibility	Funds can be spent on:	Match rate (state: individual)	Other incentives	Other conditions
Arkansas	Rapid Assets IDA	Employed. Household income less than 180% of poverty line. No more than US$10 000 assets other than house and car.	Home-ownership, post-secondary education. Starting small business.	3:1		Account holder must take 6 classes in economic literacy.
Indianapolis	Eastside Community Investments	Participant in ECI job training or skill development programmes.	Education, home ownership, materials and tools, starting a business.	9:1 up to max contribution of US$675	Initial contribution of US$250	
Texas	Central Texas Mutual Housing Association IDA Programme	Youth programmes: dependent child 17 or younger (18 if in full-time education). Account opened by parent. Alternative programme has individual opening account but parent is custodian of the account.		2:1		For accounts opened by youth he or she must be participating in the City of Austin Job Readiness Programme.
Iowa	Late 1993 the state approved a 5-year demonstration of 10 000 IDAs as part of welfare reform bill	200% of Federal poverty line or less.	Education, training, primary residence, and starting small business. Penalties for withdrawal of funds for non-approved purposes.	Variable	20% refundable tax credit on deposits. Earned interest tax deferred.	Participants can contribute a maximum of US$2 000 per year.

Source: Edwards (1997).

Evaluation of ILAs and IDAs must attempt to answer three basic questions:

- What is the *net* effects of ILAs/IDAs on savings?

- How does asset holding change behaviour? Do IDAs foster regular savings and greater expenditure on education, training, business start-up and home responsibility on the part of account holders for their own personal security and development?

- How successful have these accounts been in encouraging low income households to increase their savings?

In short, given that most IDAs target low income households, the first of these questions seeks to answer the question "Can the poor save?" while the second and third ask how successful individual accounts with government matching are in helping them to "jump start" their lives, set goals for the future and integrate themselves into the mainstream economy.

We referred to a small evaluation of a UK programme above. Two larger and more representative evaluations of IDAs are in the pipeline in the US. We concentrate on the first of these, the so-called "American Dream Demonstration" (ADD), initiated by the Center for Social Development at Washington University and the Corporation for Enterprise Development and supported by a consortium of eleven foundations.[7] Although the ADD policy demonstration is still in progress (the four-year demonstration ends in 2001, the six-year demonstration in 2003) some preliminary results are available. In the first of three proposed monitoring reports Sherraden *et al.* (2000) report on patterns of enrolment, savings and withdrawals and examine the programme and participant characteristics that are associated with savings outcomes. It must be borne in mind that these are early results, with most IDA participants having been in the programme for less than a year; it is not possible to predict how these short-term outcomes will change when participants have held accounts for longer periods.

ADD has 14 separate programmes across the country. All are run by private not-for-profit organisations; six in community development associations, the remainder in social service agencies, banks or credit unions and housing development organisations. In all 14 programmes participants earn interest on their IDA balances. The match rate varies across programmes and in some programmes it depends on either how IDA funds are used and/or on characteristics of account holders. Match rates vary from 1:1 to 7:1, with a median value of about 2:1. All programmes allow IDAs to be used (often after a mandatory minimum waiting period) for home purchase, business start-up or education. Some also permit job training and home repair and maintenance.

As of June 1999 there were 1 326 ADD account holders (the intention is to build total participants in the demonstration to about 2 000). About 90% of these were living in households with incomes below 200% of the poverty line (43% were below the poverty line). Compared to the general US population below 200% of the poverty line ADD account holders are more likely to be female, Afro-American and never married, more likely to have attended college or have a college degree and less likely to have dropped out of high school. They are also more likely to be employed and more likely to have a bank account. In short, compared to non-participants with similar income ADD participants are more likely to be disadvantaged in terms of gender, ethnicity and marital status but less disadvantaged in terms of education, employment and use of banks.

Saving outcomes

Because households on low incomes have low levels of savings[8] and, as a rule, do not or cannot save regularly, one test of the success of ILAs and IDAs is their effect on savings behaviour. Table 14 summarises the savings behaviour of ADD participants.

Table 14. **Saving outcomes in ADD programmes**

	Median	Mean	Coefficient of variation
1. Participant savings	US$181	US$286	1.08
2. Average monthly deposit	US$23	US$33	1.31
3. Deposit regularity	0.7	0.66	0.44
4. Proportion of savings goal	0.59	0.71	1.18

Notes: The figures in the table relate to outcomes across all 14 programmes.
Definitions:
1. Deposits plus interest, no matched contributions included. This is a stock measure, no account taken of length of participation.
2. Participant savings divided by months of participation, *i.e.* controls for length of time an account holder has had the opportunity to save. Again matched contributions excluded.
3. Number of months with a deposit divided by the number of months in which a deposit was possible.
4. Monthly ratio of average deposit to maximum amount eligible for matching. This ratio compares actual savings with savings behaviour that would take full advantage of the incentives offered by the programme; the typical account holder saves US$0.59 for every dollar that could be saved and matched.
Source: Sherraden *et al.* (2000).

To put these savings outcomes in some perspective it is useful to relate them to participant incomes. This is done in Table 15. Because there is no statistically significant relationship in the results between income and savings levels the saving *rate* falls as income increases. Certainly, these are quite respectable savings rates for the poor at a time when the overall personal savings rate in the US was only about 2.6% (1998-end Q1, 2000). Of course, the underlying belief of advocates of IDAs is that savings rates will grow over time, as the various features of the programmes educate actual and potential account holders about the benefits of saving. In general, the less important low income is an impediment to savings,

135|

relative to informational, cultural and institutional factors, the larger the scope for IDA-type programmes to affect savings behaviour.

These results do show that participants are willing to use their IDAs actively, although there is substantial variability across individuals as shown by the high coefficients of variation (standard deviations divided by means). The poor do save. What the results cannot tell us, of course, is the *net* effect of such programmes on savings; we do not know to what extent account holders are transferring funds from other types of saving,[9] nor the extent to which higher rates of return have an income effect which *ceteris paribus*, reduces savings.

Table 15.   **Personal savings rates in IDA programmes**
Monthly deposit as percentage of monthly household income

Income relative to poverty level	Mean	Median
0.5 and below	8.3	4.0
0.51 to 0.75	3.8	2.3
0.76 to 1.00	3.1	2.3
1.01 to 1.25	2.9	1.8
1.26 to 1.50	2.5	1.8
1.51 to 1.75	2.0	1.5
1.76 to 2.00	2.0	1.3
Over 2.00	1.7	1.4
Total	3.3	1.9

Source: Sherraden *et al.* (2000).

The evaluation also attempts to relate savings outcomes to participant characteristics and programme characteristics. This is done both using bivariate analysis and multivariate regression analysis. Using the latter approach, Table 16 highlights the variables that have statistically significant effects (at the 5% level or better), and only those variables,[10] on three of the savings outcomes in regressions including, as explanatory variables, both personal and programme characteristics.

Perhaps none of these results is particularly surprising, except perhaps the negative impact of the economics education classes that are a compulsory requirement in some IDA programmes, being intended to increase participants awareness of methods and benefits of saving. More surprising, perhaps are some of the dogs that did not bark. Amongst the personal characteristics that do not appear to be significantly associated with savings levels are income, involuntary unemployment, number of children, financial asset holding and debt levels. On the programme side the greatest surprise is the absence of the programme match rate in the group of significant[11] variables. Caution is needed here. We cannot assert that *ceteris paribus* the match rate is unimportant. In the ADD the match rate

Table 16. **Determinants of saving outcomes in ADD programmes**

	Participant savings	Average monthly deposit	Deposit regularity
Participant characteristics			
Afro-American (relative to white)	negative	negative	
Age	positive		positive
Education (relative to college graduate)	negative	negative	negative
– less than high school	negative		
– high school graduate	negative	negative	
– attended college			
Employed part-time (as opposed to full-time)			positive
Current welfare recipient		negative	
Past welfare recipient			positive
Total assets	positive		
Programme characteristics			
Age of organisation	positive		positive
Age of programme	positive		positive
Economic education hours required by programme		negative	negative
Average monthly deposit goal	positive	positive	
Prior participant affiliation with organisation	positive	positive	positive
IDA staffing level	negative		positive
IDA expenses			negative

Source: Sherraden *et al.* (2000).

is higher where population is poorest and programme savings goals are lowest. Thus the programme design will tend to generate a negative relation between the match rate and savings outcomes; the match rate is endogenous in the savings regressions.

This section concludes with an additional observation on savings by low income households. One current impediment to saving by the poor is that a large number of them are not in the banking mainstream. For example in the US, 13% of families (15% of in the US$10 000 and US$25 000 annual income bracket) do not have bank accounts. Ten million federal benefit recipients likewise are "unbanked" as are one third of all minority households. It is hard to believe that this does not have an effect on acquiring and building assets. Without bank accounts benefit recipients are paying extra for basic financial transactions such as cashing cheques and paying bills. They pay very high rates of interest for borrowing and they may find it difficult to establish credit histories. Finally, they lack access to a host of savings instruments that are taken for granted by those with bank accounts. Stegman (1999) has argued that recent moves by the US government to pay federal benefits by electronic funds transfer (EFT "99" as the programme is called), direct deposits in other words, are a first step towards greater financial inclusion. Not only does it draw the poor into the financial mainstream, but its lower costs provide financial institutions with incentives to offer low fee accounts to the group of benefit recipients. Stegman further argues that EFT and IDAs are naturally complementary; EFT brings people into the banking system and IDAs provide the incentive to use the system to the full, increasing the attractiveness of EFT benefit transfer and IDA administration to the banks.

Notes

1. Another way of stating that these countries are advanced in lifelong learning provision is to note that they have relatively small participation and expenditure gaps to close in order to fulfil OECD lifelong learning targets.

2. See the discussion of tertiary education funding in New Zealand in the previous chapter.

3. PFI has been used for construction of building such as Halls of Residence for universities. Furthermore, although not part of the PFI, the British government has employed private suppliers under performance contracts to deliver education in the compulsory schooling sector where there has been clear failure in public provision.

4. Evaluations of the British Public Finance Initiative have attempted to answer such questions *ex post.*

5. Nevertheless, voucher schemes continue to attract governments. The most recent, at the time of writing, is a plan by the Japanese government to give citizens vouchers for information technology training. The scheme has been criticised as being ill-conceived, in part because the relatively small size of the proposed voucher (Yen 6 000 *i.e.* US$55 approx.) is insufficient to pay for serious training. Nevertheless, the fact that the Japanese government is orienting its recent stimulus packages towards ICT investment does indicate a commitment to upgrading this dimension of literacy.

6. See UK Government (2001) for more details.

7. The second is the national IDA demonstration signed into law in the Assets for Independence Act (AFIA) of 1998 which will set up and help to fund approximately 50 000 IDAs. The Department of Health and Human Services has been allocated US$25 million per year for five years to run the demonstration. No results were available at the time of writing.

8. In the UK in the late 1990s, 46% of households earning less then £200 per week had no financial savings (excluding pensions and housing). 70% of lone parents had no financial savings. UK Treasury (2001), *Savings and Assets for All.*

9. However, the evaluation did establish that there was no statistical relationship between the level of non-IDA assets and savings behaviour of IDA account holders.

10. The regressions also control for gender, residence (rural/urban), marital status, unemployment status, number of children, number of adults (in household), whether bank account held, debt/income status, net worth, number of participants in actual programme, matching rates.

11. In the ADD evaluation discussed in the text, being "banked" did have a positive effect on savings outcomes. However the coefficients were not statistically significant.

Chapter 6

Policy Processes and Mechanisms

1. Rethinking skill-formation policy

Implementing a lifelong learning strategy will require careful consideration of the existing evidence about where current deficiencies lie and about which education and training policies have been successful. We have reviewed some of this evidence in preceding chapters and pointed to what we believe might constitute priority areas in the light of that evidence.

Instituting a broadly-based lifelong learning strategy will involve taking new initiatives as well as improving on existing policies. And both the new and the old will have to be accomplished with limited resources. This seems to have three broad implications for a policy approach capable of realising the lofty ambitions of what might be called the lifelong learning vision.

Firstly, there is a need to be radical and ambitious, but not over-ambitious or reckless. The so-called "imperatives" of lifelong learning will not abolish scarcity. Expensive failures will not endear lifelong learning to ministers and pressure groups arguing that extra resources are needed for the health services or transport or law and order.

Secondly, and notwithstanding the note of caution sounded above, successful implementation will inevitably involve taking some risks – on largely untried financing initiatives such as individual learning accounts for example. Naturally, these should not be undertaken recklessly. These initiatives need to be carefully thought through and efforts must be made to involve all interested parties at the planning stage; asking the social parties in any branch of lifelong learning to implement a set of new policies that they have not been involved in developing and testing is unlikely to be successful. Where feasible, pilot studies should precede full-blown implementation.

Thirdly, and related to the need to try new approaches, policy-makers will need to challenge some of the accepted ways of thinking about learning issues and about making policy. Some components of this new approach may include:

- The need to consider the menu of policies affecting individuals at different stages of the life-cycle together rather than in isolation. This is because learning is a dynamic process subject to inter-temporal synergy ("learning begets learning"). In earlier chapters we cited the effects of ECEC in improving motivation and later school achievement as a prime example of this. The need to integrate the worlds of work and of learning is another. There is ample evidence that those with more formal education receive more employer-provided training. Presumably this is because formal schooling increases the trainability of workers; training can be more ambitious because more educated workers can learn more in a given time or training courses can be shorter because the more educated learn the same thing in less time. Conversely employers are unlikely to invest in those with the lowest levels of education.

- The need to accord greater weight to non-cognitive skills such as social adaptability and motivation as opposed to purely cognitive skills as measured by test scores and formal academic qualifications.

- The need to accord greater weight to the role of families and firms in fostering relevant skills, as opposed to relying exclusively on formal educational institutions. We know that inimical family environment produces children with low motivation to succeed at school. In the light of the difficulty of attributing performance improvements to such "school quality" variables as expenditure per pupil, class size and teacher salaries, it may be the case that policies directed to families may in fact have a greater impact on school performance than these "direct" instruments. They may also be central to an effective strategy to reduce and eventually eliminate the alarmingly high rates of adult illiteracy in many OECD countries.

- The need to give greater emphasis to post-school learning. Heckman (1999) has estimated that such learning accounts for between one third and one half of all skill formation in the US. Whether or not this estimate is strictly accurate or whether it applies to other OECD countries, the fact remains that, from a lifelong learning perspective, learning by doing and other forms of workplace education deserve greater attention, relative to learning in formal educational institutions.

- The need to take a more agnostic and dynamic view of abilities rather than regard human capital formation and innate ability as independent determinants of social and economic success. While not denying that individuals differ in intrinsic abilities, it is nevertheless the case that, at least in the early years, what we often think of as ability (certainly that dimension relating to economic success) can be influenced by appropriate policies and environment.

- The need for policy to be formulated and implemented on a "joined up" basis. This follows from complementarities between different levels of education, between formal education and learning at work, and from the importance of expectations and family and social background factors in generating successful lifelong learning outcomes.

2. Setting priorities

Because there are so many different components to lifelong learning, it is obvious that it will not be feasible to devote equal amounts of resources to all of them. Nor, in general, would it be efficient to do so. So the question arises as to how priorities should be set. Is there a common sequencing of investment dictated by the underlying "technology of learning" or will priorities differ in different countries depending on history, on current bottlenecks, on political and resource constraints, etc.?

International comparisons might suggest that in some countries there are particular stages of the lifecycle (ECEC, education and training for non-academic 16-18/19 year-olds) where the level of provision is clearly short of the best practice of competitors. Here, there is a presumption that catch-up may be a priority.

More fundamentally, however, the economic answer to the question of setting priorities is that policy should aim to equalise social rates of return to different types of lifelong learning investments (each rate of return set equal to the common social discount rate). A coherent approach[1] would be to invest first in areas of lifelong learning where social rates of return were highest and work through available "projects" in descending order of rate of return until funds ran out or no further investments remained with returns in excess of the social discount rate.[2] Of course, this approach should ideally use *ex ante* not *ex post* rates of return to allocate funds, and the two may differ. One of the themes of this paper has been that, in order to meet its objectives, a lifelong learning strategy will have to seek ways of making profitable investments that have not been so in the past. Of course, it is of general interest to know which existing policies have and which have not passed rate of return tests. It would be perverse to replicate the latter unless one had clear reasons for believing that they could be made more cost-effective in the future. We have discussed various ways in which this might be achieved, from harnessing new technologies to reforming management and funding structures.

In the context of seeking ways of improving returns to currently unprofitable investments, it is worth noting some ongoing work at OECD examining the sensitivity of rate of return estimates changing some of the assumptions of the analysis.[3] The aim is to evaluate the relative importance of the different benefit and cost elements that underlie the rate of return. In turn, if governments were wishing to subsidise individual lifelong learning, such an exercise can indicate where interventions are likely to have the greatest leverage. The exercise, at its current stage of development, examines rates of return to a hypothetical 40-year-old

143

employed person who acquires the next higher level of education. To illustrate, Table 17 considers a 40-year-old male in Denmark and in the US whose highest educational attainment is upper secondary education who returns to formal education to acquire an upper tertiary qualification.[4]

Table 17.   **Sensitivity of rates of return to alternative assumptions about costs and duration of study**

Scenario	Private internal rate of return (%)	
	Denmark	USA
1. Individual bears full direct and foregone earnings costs and receives no credits which would reduce study duration.	0.7	3.8
2. Individual bears full direct and foregone earnings costs but study duration and costs halved (as credit for prior learning).	5.6	10.7
3. Individual bears direct costs but no foregone earnings costs. Full duration of study.	21.7	28.5
4. Part time study; individual pays direct costs but no foregone earnings. Duration of study is doubled.	15.9	16.9

Source: OECD education database, Secretariat calculations.

As can be seen this investment is unattractive to individuals unless where they bear the full costs and receive no credit for prior learning or experience.[5] Cutting the duration of study in half, which may be achievable if the individual is granted credit for prior learning or relevant experience or can be put on an accelerated learning programme, makes the investment more attractive (probably still marginal for the Danish man but a realistic proposition for an American man.)[6] The main source of the difference between these two returns is the halving of the foregone earnings cost. Institutional reform which recognises informal learning and grants time credit to persons studying for formal qualifications could be one method of achieving this savings. Where the whole of the foregone earnings cost can be shifted from the individual, either by part-time study as in scenario 4 or by some unspecified mechanism in scenario 3, the internal rates of return look very healthy indeed. Of course, in scenario 3 someone is bearing the foregone earnings/output cost – either the employer or the state or some combination. Thus, the social rate of return is going to be lower than the private return, but the point of the exercise is to show how such lifelong learning investments can be made more attractive to the individual investor. Naturally, if the social return is too low then it may not be worthwhile subsidising the individual.

Such a sensitivity exercise is itself sensitive to its own assumptions; in particular the effect on earnings of receiving a formal qualification at age 40.[7] Nor does it take into account any general equilibrium effects on relative earnings that may follow if generous subsidies were offered to large numbers of poorly qualified workers. Nevertheless, the exercise does have value, and will have even more as the numbers are refined in the process of further analysis. The exercise emphasises the point made above that rates of return are not written in stone, but can be used to highlight where educational "bottlenecks" occur and suggest what factors must be targeted to remove them.

Even where we make allowances for reforms which may be expected to change *ex ante* rates of return, the requirement that marginal rates of return be equalised in different expenditure is unlikely to be operational in setting priorities for a broadly-based lifelong learning strategy. This is partly because rates of return have not been estimated for all components of a lifelong learning policy package. Rates of return have been widely calculated for the different levels of formal education, some have been cited in previous chapters. Sometimes such estimates have influenced policy formation, although not necessarily decisively in all cases. The same cannot be said for other aspects of lifelong learning. This is partly because economic and policy interest is relatively recent (as is the case with ECEC) and/or because rate of return analysis is less feasible, or the results are less reliable, in these areas than is the case with formal education. Work-related training is a case in point; the evaluation methodology is evolving, and although we know a lot more about how to evaluate programmes, there are still many unanswered questions. In discussing the high rates of return to the Perry Programme and similar specifically targeted high quality ECEC interventions in the US, we warned that it was difficult to extrapolate the results to similar, but not identical, programmes targeted at different populations. In general, rate of return and other forms of programme evaluation are plagued by the non-availability of data, the heterogeneous nature of provision, the often informal nature of provision (as in many types of in-service training), the small scale of some demonstration programmes, etc.

In the light of the point made above about the importance of non-cognitive outcomes of lifelong learning programmes, another shortcoming of existing evaluation methods, including rate of return analysis, is the overwhelming concentration on the development of cognitive skills. Thus, evaluation of educational interventions on the basis of their contribution to test scores or formal qualifications may underestimate the true returns if these take the form of improved non-cognitive skills of the affected groups.

Standard rate of return analysis tells us that, *ceteris paribus*, both social and private rates of return will be lower for older than for younger persons. The main reason for this is that the "payback period" over which the investment returns accrue is shorter for older persons. Secondly, if learning does beget learning, then this type of return will be lower for investments made later in life. Thirdly, while remedial

145|

programmes may be called for when individuals fail to develop functional literacy or whose skills have been made obsolete by technical change, it is much more cost-effective to deal with at least some of these problems before individuals reach the labour market. And because employers give more training to better educated workers, improving basic education may be the most effective way of encouraging employer provided training.

These considerations suggest that there is a strong presumption that reallocating funds from investment in older persons to investing in the young will be efficient. Under such a scenario, displaced older workers would receive income support or employers could be subsidised if they continue to employ them, but no major allocation of public funds would be devoted to retraining them. We have argued that this may be a short-sighted approach, given the relatively early ages at which men, in particular, are leaving the workforce. The public expenditure costs of passively supporting such a large group of workers, especially as the effects of ageing populations will continue well into the new century, could well be prohibitive. If the rapid introduction of new technologies into the workplace in general leads to more and more frequent retraining, a central plank of a lifelong learning policy could be to provide incentives to individuals and firms for older workers to partake in this process. If for no other there are strong equity reasons not to marginalise older people by essentially removing them from the workplace.

Equity considerations will temper many decisions and perhaps give the green light to policies that would fail a strict rate of return test. However, equity can never justify poor projects; for example, if particular government training programmes are ineffectual in increasing the labour market success of trainees, it is hard to see how such programmes could be justified on equity grounds. Apart from standard equity arguments that we considered above, such as the affordability of quality ECEC and the optimal degree of cost sharing in tertiary education, there will be many other less obvious aspects of equity to be considered in devising funding mechanisms for lifelong learning. Under existing methods of subsidisation does the vocational stream do less well than the academic stream? Do mothers who stay at home to raise children do as well in terms of government policy as those who go out to work? If not, is the distortion intentional? If so, how is it justified? Are small firms at a disadvantage with regard to providing work-related training compared with large firms?[8] Other examples abound.

3. Auditing existing policies

Not all policy to promote lifelong learning is new. Many existing labour market and education programmes are likely to be on the right track. Previous chapters identified some of these in the ECEC fields, and in training programmes. Governments are already responding to the findings on adult illiteracy by tilting education strategy to become more skills-based. Some welfare-to-work programmes offer job-based training of the type that should address some of the lifelong learning needs of school to work transitions and cater to older worker populations.

A prime area that would require reviewing, if governments were seriously to accord high priority to lifelong learning, is the tax system. As well as looking at tax incentives for individual lifelong learning components such as training, it is necessary to consider whether in overall terms the tax system achieves the desired balance between:

- Human capital and physical capital accumulation.

- Human capital investments by high skilled and wealthy workers on the one hand and low skilled, poorer workers on other.

- On-the-job investments in human capital and investments in formal schooling.

- Human capital investments at different phases of the life cycle.

A high marginal tax rate reduces the net return to working and extra hour (day) and, by the same token, reduces the opportunity cost of spending a marginal hour in school or other human capital investment activity which keeps the investor out of the labour market. But the high marginal tax rate also reduces the marginal return of a human capital augmented earnings increase. Thus flat rate labour taxes will be neutral where the only costs are foregone earnings. Even with flat rate taxes an increase in the rate will discourage human capital investments where there are non-deductible out of pocket expenses as well as opportunity costs because the returns fall proportionately more than the costs. Where direct costs of human capital investment are either very small or are themselves deductible, increases in the tax rate would be neutral and human capital would be a desirable base for tax increases because such increases would be non-distorting. Under a progressive tax system, however, this result does not hold. If the earnings gain from human capital investments is taxed at a higher rate than the foregone earnings (the earnings gain puts the individual into a higher marginal tax bracket), then human capital investment is discouraged relative to a flat rate system.

Taxes on interest income can affect investment in both physical and human capital, but the effects may not be predictable. Tax cuts that increase the after tax interest rate reduce the incentive to invest in human capital (discounted returns are lower). They may, however, increase the return to physical capital, increasing investment and, in the longer run, wages (as the additional physical capital increases labour productivity). Whether all wages are increased in roughly the same proportion or not will depend on, amongst other things, the extent of capital-skill complementarity.

Does the tax system favour (or discourage) human capital investment equally for all individuals? Not necessarily. In the US, for example, individuals cannot now

147|

deduct interest paid on educational loans. However, mortgage interest payments are deductible. This enables families with housing equity to take out mortgages to finance the education of their children. This favours those on higher incomes who are more likely to be home owners, and constitutes another argument against the granting of tax relief on mortgage interest payments. Not only does it favour those on higher incomes directly but it can also subsidise the education of their children.

Many other details of the tax system can affect aspects of lifelong learning investments. For example the US tax system tends to favour on-the-job training rather than training away from the workplace, and the tax treatment of off-the-job training is more favourable where it is financed by employers than when it is not. All in all, employer provided training is favoured over training undertaken independently.

In other areas it may be possible to reform accounting and valuation practices at relatively low cost in such a way as to increase the profitability of existing investments and/or increase investments. Formal and informal training by firms is a case in point. We have alluded elsewhere to the inherent uncertainty of the returns to firm financed training; trainees may quit, product demand may change, the effect on productivity may differ from that expected when training decisions are taken, etc. However, in addition to these uncertainties it is arguable that current accounting and valuation methods inadequately reflect the likely benefits of training. In such circumstances investors will have little knowledge of firms' training efforts and stock market valuations will not adequately reflect such investments. In fact, training is generally treated as a current expense in company accounts rather than amortised as an investment. By the same token firms' stocks of human capital do not appear on the balance sheets of corporations (nor in the national accounts as part of national wealth). It is true of course that human capital differs in one important respect of a firm's physical assets – it is not owned by the firm. However, long-term relationships between workers and firms are common, even in today's labour markets, and indeed firms providing training have an interest in providing incentives for such long-term attachments. This makes it not unreasonable that information on the human capital embodied in a firm's labour force should be reflected in information on its asset structure. The failure to adequately measure and value human capital generates a major lacuna in the information available both for those with responsibility for training programmes within firms and to potential outside investors in these firms. In short, human capital tends to be outside the common information set that informs investment and lending decisions. With respect to lifelong learning, this is likely to result in managers facing reduced incentives to devote resources to training. Furthermore, resource allocation across firms is likely to be distorted because, in selecting firms or sectors in which to invest, neither institutional nor individual investors have sufficient information to select firms making major investments in such as general or specific human capital. There is also an element of the public goods problem here: better accounting procedures would benefit all firms, but no individual firms have the incentive to incur the costs of developing new information systems on their own.

A recent report from the Brookings Institution (Blair and Wallman, 2001) makes a number of recommendations, which would put intangible assets on a similar footing with tangible assets. Two of these are particularly germane to the lifelong learning context, in that they could lead to firms providing more, and more efficient, training to their employees:

- *Data building.* Governments should fund or part-fund a project to define and assemble new types of information to enable the private sector to construct "new business models and metrics" appropriate to the knowledge economy, where intangibles are increasingly important. Such a project would require national institutions (in the US candidates include the Bureau of Economic Analysis, the Department of Commerce, the Census Bureau and the Bureau of Labor Statistics) to collaborate with private sector firms and corporations.

- *Corporate disclosure.* Indicators of human as well as physical capital and investment in people as well as in machines need to be developed which should then be included in the disclosures required for publicly traded companies. While some companies have made tentative voluntary steps in this direction the report believes more needs to be done and that the element of compulsion is required. In the US such developments come within the responsibilities of the Securities and Exchange Commission and the Financial Accounting Standards Board.

4. Cross-cutting issues

By its very nature lifelong learning calls for new ways of thinking about policy. In particular, because it involves such diverse activities and a wide range of interested parties, it is unlikely that appropriate policies can be formulated and implemented within any one government, department or agency. This means that co-ordination and interdependence in policy-making assume particular importance. Family policy, tax policy and workplace issues will assume equal importance with purely educational aspects.

One imperative, given the complex and diverse challenges that a lifelong learning strategy has to confront, is to prevent policy thinking becoming too narrowly focused. It is unlikely that a narrow "departmental" approach will suffice. A national literacy and numeracy strategy is probably a good example of the need for a cross-cutting approach. The objectives are sufficiently diverse to require contributions from, and co-ordination between, several government departments and organisations. For example, raising school standards, while partly about the level

149|

and allocation of school inputs, may have as much to do with alleviating child poverty and addressing other aspects of the child's learning environment.

In principle, policy-makers with responsibility for lifelong learning need to perform an audit across existing programmes – tax and social security programmes and industrial policy as well as education and training programmes, to see whether they are "lifelong learning-friendly". If not, they can ask whether it would be possible to tilt them more in this way without compromising the main objectives of the programmes.

This method of thinking about policy in a more "joined up" way, along with other public service management techniques such as the use of performance indicators, public service agreements and the like, is becoming more common. In the UK, the Treasury has conducted 15 "cross-cutting" reviews in areas such as services for the under-5s, welfare-to-work, drugs, crime, young people at risk, old people, ECEC, science and research. In each review individual spending departments, the Treasury, Cabinet Office and outside experts are involved. Such reviews have led, in some cases, to service agreements across departments and pooled budgets.

While the logic of cross-cutting initiatives is compelling, making them succeed is likely to be difficult. Issues that are difficult to manage within single organisations or departments (stakeholder involvement, risk management, etc.) are even more so across traditional departmental boundaries. To put it crudely there can simply be "too many cooks". Such difficulties might be avoided if there are clear lines of authority, clear objectives and, probably, a single senior co-ordinator.

Notes

1. There may be some exceptions dictated by resource constraints and/or by the lumpiness of investments.

2. The argument is framed in terms of lifelong learning investments simply because that is our subject. It should be obvious that policy-makers would have to treat *all* potential investments in the same way; there is no justification for treating lifelong learning investments as a special case. Where non-lifelong learning investments have higher rates of return, these should be undertaken first.

3. OECD Secretariat calculations based on a re-analysis of data used to calculate internal rates of return to formal education; results of the original calculations were published in OECD (1998), pp. 360-363.

4. The exercise also considers female rates of return and rates of return to acquiring a university degree. Other countries and further variations in the scenarios are also analysed.

5. This is essentially for the reasons highlighted in Box 2 headed "Effect on private returns of delaying human capital investments" in Chapter 4.

6. These statements are somewhat imprecise because to know whether a given internal rate of return signals a profitable investment or not we need to know the individual's discount/borrowing rate. An investment is worthwhile when the internal rate of return exceeds this comparison rate.

7. There are also likely to be selection issues which, if ignored, could bias results. Are those who voluntarily undertake formal education at age 40 more able and ambitious than other 40-year-olds who choose not to upgrade their qualifications? If so such individuals may in any case have higher earnings. This increases opportunity costs of investments but may also increase the benefits of further education above the average level.

8. There exists fairly robust evidence that employees in large firms are more likely to receive employer provided training which suggests that economies of scale may exist in the provision of such training. In such circumstances, there may be grounds for interventions which promote group training or offering employees of small firms subsidised access to public training programmes, provided these are responsive to the needs of small firms.

Annex

Summary of Proceedings of the International Conference "Lifelong Learning as an Affordable Investment"

6-8 December 2000, Château Laurier
Ottawa, Canada

1. Background and purpose of the conference

Making lifelong learning for all a reality poses a particularly complex resource challenge because, in contrast to other far-reaching education reforms, it changes so many parameters at once. It implies quantitative expansion of learning opportunities; qualitative changes in the content of existing learning activities; qualitatively and quantitatively different learning activities and new settings; and changes in the timing of learning activities in the lifecycle of individuals. These developments imply, in turn, a strong likelihood of increases in the total outlays by society for education, training and learning activities, as well as changes in the relative costs of providing and participating in such activities. Constraints on, and competition for, public resources combined with the presence of substantial private returns to certain aspects of lifelong learning imply a need to increase the private share of the overall finance burden.

To implement strategies for lifelong learning, policy-makers and social partners need to address three resource questions:

- What resources are likely to be required in order to make lifelong learning for all a reality?
- Under what conditions can the mandate be made more affordable to society?
- What is the role of public policy in helping to meet those conditions?

The Organisation for Economic Co-operation and Development and Human Resources Development Canada organised an International Conference on Lifelong Learning as an Affordable Investment, in order to provide a forum in which public policy-makers, employers, and trade unions could address these questions. The conference drew on analyses, findings, and lessons from different components of the Organisation's work on financing lifelong learning, as well as relevant material from the Organisation's thematic reviews on early childhood education and care, transitions from learning to work, tertiary education, and adult learning. It also drew on information provided by participants concerning recent initiatives and policies.

2. Setting the stage

The conference was opened by Claire Morris, Deputy Minister for Human Resources Development Canada and John Martin, Director for Education, Employment, Labour and Social Affairs at the OECD. They underlined the importance of human capital to economic performance, social cohesion, and individual development, and, as a consequence, the critical role that lifelong learning has the potential to play in upgrading and renewing human capital. However, they stressed the necessity of making lifelong learning an affordable investment in order to fulfil that potential and transform "lifelong learning for all from a neat political slogan to a strategy that is both *feasible* and *consequential*".

John Martin argued that lifelong learning was likely to require substantial net new resources to be fully implemented. But the level of resources needed was subject to how ambitiously or how modestly government and social partners defined lifelong learning. In view of the limited options for expanding public expenditure and the presence of private returns to learning, in the form of higher wages and increased productivity, the requirements for net new resources need to be met by both the public and private sector. This requires a dialogue among government, employers and trade unions unlike that usually associated with education and training policy, because it is centred on financing *partnership*. The speakers noted that the conference was intended to facilitate such a dialogue. If the eventual divisions of financial responsibility are to be sustainable, the incentives for the different social partners to invest in lifelong learning need to be strengthened. John Martin sketched out results of work in progress at the OECD that suggested that stronger incentives depended on achieving important changes in institutional arrangements, particularly with regard to factors that affect the duration of learning activities. Participants were encouraged to identify strategies for reducing costs and increasing the benefits from learning activities.

3. How is lifelong learning transforming the debate over resources for learning?

In the opening plenary panel[1] of the conference, speakers representing governmental, research, employer, and trade unions presented their respective views on how the usual debates associated with decisions affecting resources for learning are transformed when learning is viewed over a lifelong perspective. Although "lifelong learning" cuts across the life-cycle from cradle to grave, the resource and financing issues vary in their nature and importance at different points in the life-cycle. Panellists were in broad agreement with the public-good rationale for state financing. Pre-school, elementary and secondary education, and training for the unemployed and persons at-risk generated social returns that are sufficient to justify state support in these areas. Beyond that, at the level of tertiary education and continuing education and training by employed persons, learning generates substantial private returns that justify private actors assuming a greater share of costs.

With that consensus view as a starting point, panellists argued that "lifelong learning" and the general societal perceptions about the importance of learning are introducing cross currents if not outright contradictions in the debate over resources at different levels.

Representatives of employers and trade unions shared the view that governments have prime responsibility for initial education through the secondary level, and learning opportunities for the unemployed and at-risk adults with low levels of qualifications. Against that background of social partner consensus, public policies are mixed. In Canada, public education budgets are being cut and private financing of schools is on the increase at the same time that (and, possibly, because) public debate over learning issues is overshadowed by the debate over health care and tax cuts. In contrast, the United Kingdom has moved from state provision of secondary education to experiment with state-provided allowances for individuals to continue post-secondary studies. In the United States, though the Department of Education remains focused on the learning needs of the excluded, unemployment insurance funds increasingly are available for training employed workers.

Views were more diverse with regard to learning opportunities later in the life-cycle. Virtually everyone agreed that learning opportunities for adults need to be expanded. It was argued from the trade union side that adults already cover many of the direct and indirect costs of the learning activities that already are available. Adults contribute to financing through out-of-pocket spending as well as foregone leisure and, sometimes, earnings. Expansion of opportunities should not replace existing employer- or state-funded opportunities, but should supplement them. Moreover, opportunities should expand in such a way as to encourage efficiency in provision (lower cost) and more choice for individuals, possibly through mechanisms such as individual learning accounts. The employer representative emphasised the importance of sharing the financing burden of learning activities – new activities as well as those that already exist – through shared use of vocational facilities and other educational facilities where substantial investment in ICT may be needed. Increased investment should be encouraged through stronger incentives for each of the multiple partners, rather than regulation. Though small- and medium-size enterprises (SMEs) provide less formal training, they provide considerable non-formal skill development that can be captured through assessment of prior learning.

Whatever is done, all participants agreed that there is a second challenge, over and above increasing the overall level of resources for learning, and that is reaching poorly qualified persons who are under-represented in learning activities. While panellists noted the importance of adapting to the learning needs of poorly qualified persons, the lack of time for training and its costs were seen as major barriers.

The question of who should finance the net increase in resources for learning among adults was surprisingly non-controversial. There was broad agreement on the principle that employers and employees should share the bulk of the burden, that government has responsibility for much of the cost for poorly qualified and indigent individuals. What was not so clear was *by what means* financial responsibilities might be shared. Remedies mentioned included learning accounts and other mechanisms to empower learners to "shop" for learning opportunities, and recognition of informal learning both to reduce the time required for training by eliminating duplicative learning, and to increase the confidence of learners and their appetite for learning.

4. Resource and finance issues as they emerge in different sectors of lifelong learning

Addressing the attendant resource implications risks opening a complex debate because, ultimately, the scope of the mandate can touch everything from the workplace, to the home, to leisure activities, as well as formal education. The conference organisers chose therefore to focus on the finance and resource issues that arise in the immediate and near term in connection with strengthening opportunities for lifelong learning in *existing institutional arrangements* for four "sectors" in which learning presently occurs: early childhood, compulsory and upper-secondary education, tertiary education, and the workplace and other settings for adult learning.

For each of the sectors, participants addressed the following four issues:

- How does lifelong learning affect past assumptions and practices regarding who pays for learning?
- How does lifelong learning increase the opportunity for enhancing cost-effectiveness of providing learning, and increasing its benefits?
- What is being done to mobilise financial resources for lifelong learning?
- What mechanisms and processes make it easier to address the resource issues that cut across ministries and the public and private sectors?

Researchers, public officials, and representatives of employers and trade unions from more than 20 countries presented and discussed evidence on how these issues were being addressed. Sector-by-sector discussions were held in workshops. These were followed by debate in plenary sessions over priorities and next steps. The rest of this chapter reviews the highlights of these presentations and debates. For more details and documentation on the conference see *www.oecd.org*.

Early childhood education and care

The central resource and finance issue at this level is the need to achieve higher levels of public investment. It was argued that public investment can be justified on the grounds that intervention at this stage in the lifecycle generates social capital. In arguing the need for ECEC, Naomi Karp,[2] chair of the workshop, cited the role that such programmes play in preventing poor school performance (4 out of 10 third graders in the United States have reading difficulties; nearly half of all children entering kindergarten have social or attention problems). She also noted that though 70% of US mothers work, high quality care for young children is almost non-existent. Early childhood interventions yield substantial and lasting benefits in the form of cognitive development, early health care, improved subsequent school performance, and productive and participative citizens. Fraser Mustard[3] pointed out the important role that such interventions can play when complemented by good parenting. Availability of institutional arrangements for early childhood education and care also facilitate increases in labour force participation of women and family earnings. Because of the substantial social returns, it was strongly argued that capacity needs to be increased in order to extend opportunities to all families that want them.

But the substantial benefits to society do not ensure that universal (or greatly expanded) ECEC will be an affordable public investment. First, quality is essential, but it is expensive. Barbara Martin-Korpi[4] estimated that places in municipal-run centres cost on average SEK 56 200 per child (about US$5 460), though lower cost options are available in non-municipal centres and parental-run centres. Naomi Karp cited costs of roughly US$5 690 in the US. However, even these figures do not reflect full costs of policies for young children. In countries where interventions are well developed, they are not seen as replacing strong parental presence for young children. Barbara Martin-Korpi noted that one-year-olds were not enrolled in centre-based care in Sweden because of parental leave policy that guaranteed 80% of a parent's salary for a period of 15 months. Kirsten Eknes[5] noted that Norway has an optional cash benefit of US$320 per month per child under age 3 for parents who choose to keep their young children at home instead of enrolling them in ECEC institutions.

Generally, it would appear that there are only limited prospects in the medium-term for cost containment and improved efficiency in the provision of ECEC. In some countries the sector is relatively new and still in a state of flux with regard to the number of children served and the number of providers. The momentum for expansion is strong. As Marta Morgan[6] said, ECEC is seen as a social imperative. But the understanding of what works best, for whom, and under what conditions – the kind of knowledge that is needed in order to improve cost-effectiveness of ECEC programmes and policies – is limited, surprisingly so in the view of some observers. Donald Verry[7] and Abrar Hasan[8] underlined the importance of building evidence of what works in ECEC and its social and economic benefits, and increasing understanding of how to provide ECEC on a cost-effective basis.

The most radical approach to improving cost-effectiveness is being pursued in the Netherlands, and that is to create more open markets for child care. Frans de Vjilder[9] outlined the strategy in the Netherlands, which is to get government out of the role of supplying

ECEC, and into the role of helping parents as consumers of ECEC. This involves reducing direct public support to ECEC institutions, through the tax system, shifting it into the hands of parents. By 2002, the central government will end the subsidies to municipalities for ECEC provision. Some municipalities already are providing subsidies to parents to purchase ECEC services from private providers. In order to ensure quality of private provision, the government is requiring such providers to meet quality standards.

In at least some countries, the goal of expanding capacity of ECEC seems unachievable without some non-public contribution. In Sweden, where 75% of pre-school children participate, parents now pay 17% of the cost; this is up from 10% in 1992. Municipalities have introduced income-tested schedules of fees to be paid by parents. The government has introduced a bill that would guarantee 15 hours per week free participation for all children; beyond that, parents would pay fees on a sliding scale based on family income. Frans de Vijlder noted that in the Netherlands, where institutional capacity for ECEC is more limited, the policy is to rely more on non-governmental sources of income. In 1988, the government committed to double the number of child care places through funding on a partnership basis, with government contributing 35%, parents 44%, and employers 21%. It is planned that eventually the financing burden will be re-balanced with each of the partners paying one third. While government and employers each will pay one-third, low income parents will pay less, and higher income parents will pay more. In contrast, authorities in Norway are hoping to increase capacity *and* reduce the share of ECEC costs paid by parents by increasing the financial contribution by central and local government; however, it is not certain that the additional public resources are available for such a policy.

One factor that complicates ECEC policy-making in general, and finance and resource issues in particular, is the fact that responsibility for ECEC frequently is divided across ministries, and across levels of government. In Sweden, policy in this area was developed on a collaborative basis with labour market authorities. But, in order to ensure that ECEC was well-linked with education policy, responsibilities were consolidated in the Ministry of Education. Decisions about the allocation of resources for ECEC are made at the local level by municipal authorities; such decisions are guided by common guidelines. But such uniformity probably is exceptional, if only because of the extensive experience – more than 30 years – with ECEC. In Norway responsibilities for ECEC rest with the Ministry of Children and Family Affairs – separate from education. As there is a strong tradition for local delivery of public services, counties and municipalities have the principal responsibilities for financing ECEC centres, with financial resources that come from the central government but are ear-marked for ECEC. The Netherlands transition to funding the consumers rather than the providers of ECEC may make resource allocation more straightforward, but a more definite result will have to wait until that approach is more fully implemented. Another example is represented by the kind of experience seen in Canada as described by Sharon Manson-Singer,[10] where a nationwide National Child Benefit has been introduced for all-low income families. That has opened the way for a National Children's Agenda and a federal/provincial/territorial Early Childhood initiative, under which governments have agreed to invest incrementally in ECEC. Almost inevitably, the priorities of governments and their capacity to finance such initiatives will vary across provinces. Parents continue to shoulder the largest share of the financial burden.

Schools

Schools, as the heart of initial education, are seen as being the financial responsibility of government. In the context of debate about resources and financing of lifelong learning, therefore, workshop chair Annelise Hauch[11] outlined the core issue as being how to get the

157|

"most" out of the public resources that are allocated to education. Charles Ungerleider[12] as well as Torkel Alfthan[13] reinforced the message about the necessity of substantial public support, arguing that investments in primary and secondary education saved government money by reduced economic dependency, improved use of health care, and reduced criminal activity. He also made the point that the cost of providing a sound initial education was far less than the cost of remedial measures for adults. But this leaves the question of how publicly financed schools can achieve cost-effective provision of quality schooling, while ensuring equitable access to quality schooling.

Patrick Brunier[14] framed the issue today as being not necessarily one of *more* resources as much as an issue of *better use* of existing resources. Frans de Vijlder identified "choice" as the main feature of the strategies followed in the Netherlands in order to achieve these objectives. This policy is pursued by allowing any group of parents to start a school and receive financial support equal to that provided to public schools. As a result, 70% of schools are administered by private boards. However, after World War II it became clear that equal treatment for different socio-economic groups did not yield equal outcomes. This prompted new initiatives in the 1960s and 1970s to provide compensatory resources to offset disadvantages experienced by some groups. Extra payments were directed to schools serving disadvantaged groups, and to schools located in disadvantaged geographical areas. However, it would appear that there are limits to how much such a policy of choice leads to greater effective choice or, ultimately, improved quality. First, choice is effectively limited because once groups sharing religion, ethnicity, or social values start a school, there can be considerable pressure for students to stay in the school. Second, quality has not been improved noticeably, perhaps partly because diversity *within* schools has suffered. Furthermore, even where resources allowed smaller class size, there was little impact on quality. Sarah Elson-Rogers,[15] while acknowledging the importance of non-financial factors, such as curriculum, noted that some countries were using changes in financing strategies to drive quality improvement. Denmark introduced the "taxi-meter" scheme as a device for allocating financial resources on a per-student basis; this gives institutions the incentive to control costs (they retain the difference between actual per-student costs and the taxi-meter rate), while improving quality (in order to attract students in a system in which students can go to the school of their choice). Eivind Heder[16] reported that in Norway, where the recently adopted *Competence Reform* guarantees poorly qualified adults the right to return to primary and secondary education, it is expected that flexibility in provision combined with greater readiness and motivation on the part of adults to learn, will reduce the time required for learning, relative to the time required in the regular school programme. But Veronica Lacey,[17] reflecting on experience in Canada, raised the question as to whether it was possible to reconcile standardisation of teaching methods to reduce costs, with greater individualisation of education in order to sustain and raise retention rates. Anders Vind[18] also questioned whether strategies adopted in some countries to raise cost-effectiveness of education by financing institutions on the basis of outcomes might lead to "creaming" – providers excluding high-risk would-be students in order to reduce failure rates.

Tertiary education

Participation in tertiary education has exploded in many countries. In those countries where participation was already high, enrolments have been sustained or creep higher still. In this climate, the financial and resource issues take two general forms:

- How to shift the burden of financing so that government does not pay the full costs of expanded enrolments.
- How to allocate public resources in such a way as to create incentives for more cost-effective provision and/or financing partnerships.

Developments in New Zealand provide probably the clearest examples of policies oriented in these directions. John Scott[19] outlined the three goals of the new funding arrangements: increase participation, innovation, and efficiency. Policies are fashioned to achieve these goals by shifting state support from institutions to individuals, in order to move towards a "demand-driven" system. Institutions, which have been forced to increase tuition fees by nearly NZ$ 3 000 (about US$1 300), are given autonomy in deciding how to attract students, and how to increase efficiency enough to keep fee increases to a minimum. In order to minimise the inequities of increasing the financial burden of students, public support for higher education has been shifted to the students (demand side) through tuition subsidies paid to full-time students and student loans whose repayment is income contingent. Evaluations of the results to date of the initiatives are mixed. Participation in tertiary education has risen, and it has risen for persons from all socio-economic status groups. But the shift in financing mechanisms does not appear to be neutral with respect to impact on the content of tertiary education. The high fees combined with an attempt to create a demand-driven system have led students to focus more on courses of study that lead to employment: enrolments are up in law and accounting, and down in philosophy. Institutions are driven more by increasing enrolments, than by producing graduates; in the short term this might lead to a misallocation of resources within institutions away from activities that might improve retention or better meet the needs of students already enrolled.

Reforms in other countries have been more limited in the scope of their objectives and instruments. One objective has been to make expansion of tertiary enrolments more affordable by improving efficiency of institutions. Annika Persson[20] noted that in Sweden tertiary education still is tuition free with the state still channelling resources for tertiary education directly to the institutions. In order to make the system more demand driven, institutions are encouraged to increase efficiency by being paid according to the number of full-time students they enrol through completion. Enrolments have increased by 60% since 1990. But Persson underlined the importance of addressing the costs of living as well as the scarcity of time (another facet of financial barriers when it is seen as the cost of replacing foregone earnings) in order to ensure access. Elie Cohen[21] noted that in France there is a heavy emphasis on encouraging innovation in tertiary education as a way of dealing with the financial pressures imposed by rising enrolments. He and an expert from Hungary mentioned assessment of prior learning as another way of reducing costs. But there also is pressure on regional government to contribute more. Hyunsook Yu[22] argued that efficiencies gained through increased student-instructor ratios did not necessarily undermine quality, thanks to technological improvements in instructional methods as well as greater reliance on non-conventional learning environments. However, Paul Davenport,[23] while acknowledging that the impact of student-faculty ratios on educational quality was subject to debate, stated his opinion that recent increases in student-faculty ratios had already had a significant negative impact on the quality of university education in Canada, and that further increases would be inimical to the university environment for research and scholarly innovation, activities that are vital to a knowledge economy. He also stressed that rising student-faculty ratios reduce the capacity of universities to equip graduates with the communication, team-work, and critical thinking skills needed in a knowledge economy. He noted also that with growing graduate enrolments at major universities, significant new faculty hiring would be essential to ensure not only appropriate student-faculty ratios but that faculty were available for the intensive one-on-one work which is part of graduate training.

Perhaps the most vexed issue treated in the workshop concerned the importance of finance issues relative to other issues in determining *access* to tertiary, and the precise way in

159|

which they influence access. Participants broadly agreed that the presence or absence of fees were not decisive in determining who participates. What is probably more important is the extent to which the associated costs of living can be covered and, where such costs are financed through loans, how students and their families view indebtedness. Though grants are available to cover some of the costs of living, it appears that governments rely increasingly on *loans* to finance cost of living and thereby facilitate access to an increasingly large number of students. John Scott and David Stewart[24] noted that New Zealand and Scotland rely increasingly on loans for which repayment is income contingent, *i.e.*, for which repayment is required only when a graduate's income exceeds a certain level.

But is loan-financed assistance likely to fundamentally alter the accessibility of tertiary education? After all, as Raymond Ivany[25] and others pointed out, increases in tertiary participation tend to favour individuals from high socio-economic backgrounds. In this regard there seem to be reasons for doubts. A number of presenters, as well participants in the general discussion, made the point that increased reliance on loans to finance direct and indirect costs of tertiary education was leading to an increase in student indebtedness that fell disproportionately on students from families with lower socio-economic backgrounds (and who have fewer financial resources). Means-tested repayment loans reduce the risk that indebtedness becomes burdensome. But Stefan Wolter[26] pointed out that individuals from disadvantaged social groups tend to have higher time preferences for money (and would therefore require a higher expected rate of return than others before investing). It was not clear from the evidence presented in the workshop whether such loan strategies would raise expected rates of return to tertiary education to a sufficiently high level to compensate for such higher time preferences and increase participation of lower socio-economic individuals in tertiary education. Workshop chairman Thomas Townsend[27] noted the policy environment in which tertiary education costs were being shifted from government to individuals. He underlined the importance of evaluating the distributional impacts of such shifts and understanding better the limits of cost-sharing.

Adult and workplace learning

In contrast to other sectors in which lifelong learning occurs, in the discussion of adult and workplace learning there was little consideration given to the question of public investment in learning. Rather, the resource issues were defined principally in terms of how to increase employers and employee investment in learning, and how to address the problem of under-investment in learning particularly by less qualified individuals. Workshop chair Joxerramon Bengoetxea[28] noted the importance of identifying mechanisms that would allow the financing burden to be shared among the different relevant actors.

It was argued that one approach to increasing private sector investment in training was to put in place systems for the assessment and recognition of skills and competences acquired outside formal education systems. Angel Calderón[29] summarised results of an evaluation of the National System of Skills Testing and Certification that has been implemented in Mexico. This system was put in place in order to make it possible to certify skills and competences of experienced workers, thus obviating the need (time and cost) of enrolling in formal training programmes to obtain qualifications corresponding to such skills. It was found that although employers were not willing to pay the cost of evaluating and certifying skills and competences acquired through experience, they would use such information in hiring and wage setting decisions. Individuals were willing to pay at least some of the costs because certification reduced the risk of unemployment and the cost of job search by making skills more visible and transferable. In commenting on the Mexican experience, Nicholas Fox[30] stressed the importance of establishing credible procedures for defining and measuring skills; he noted results of a related experience in the UK in which individuals were far more likely to participate in private sector training programme because its certification procedures were seen as more credible than a similar public sector programme.

While this first strand of the workshop discussion focused on strategies for reducing certain *economic* costs of lifelong learning for adults, the second strand centred on shifting and sharing the *financial* costs of adult learning. In this regard Lil Ljunggren Lönnberg[31] outlined a proposal developed in Sweden for the creation of individual learning accounts as a mechanism for facilitating investment in lifelong learning by experienced adults. The initiative, which was to be presented to the Swedish government the following week, follows up on earlier government initiatives to expand and strengthen opportunities for community-based adult education, labour market and in-service training, advanced vocational training, and other non-work education. The learning account initiative is aimed to establish a financing mechanism that increases *individual choice* in training decisions by providing a basis for *co-financing* such costs. The accounts are intended to make it easier for individuals to acquire the financial resources needed to cover *direct* as well as *indirect* costs by reducing the cost of capital to finance such expenditure. In particular, it is intended to make it more financially feasible for individuals to pursue studies that may require them to withdraw from employment, or that employers might not be willing to support because they are not related to an individual's immediate job. This would be done by allowing individuals to set aside pre-tax earnings in a learning account; resources allocated for direct expenses would be tax deductible; resources drawn to replace income during training would be treated as ordinary income. The Swedish authorities are likely to implement some form of the initiative because of the belief that increased learning benefits individuals, employers, and society; the evidence of popular interest in pursuing more learning; and the concern that presently individuals' motivation and means to learn are constrained by a lack of financial resources.

Another presentation on individual learning accounts considered results of a pilot project that ran between 1996 and 1999. Kay Cheesman[32] reported on the experience with an initiative organised by the local training authority in Gloucestershire, in collaboration with a financial institution. These accounts were established as mechanisms to stimulate learning activity on the part of low income individuals who, as a group, tended to participate less in education and training than others. Although the accounts were similar to regular savings plans, an account entitled the holder to discounts on education material and course fees, as well as a lump-sum contribution by the local training authority. Employers also could contribute. Although there was no "control group" that could serve as a basis for comparison, a survey of account holders indicated that the initiative succeeded in reaching a population that typically is under-represented in adult learning activities (those with low and moderate incomes, females, those with little education and training after initial education), and in increasing motivation to participate in further education and training.

François Duranleau[33] reported the results of initiatives in Québec with a different focus, namely on encouraging employers to invest more in learning activity. A number of measures were tried after it was discovered in the early 1980s that employers were investing little in training. They were based on persuasion (government encouraging employers to invest in training), carrots (tax credits for training) and sticks (train-or-pay tax levy). On balance it would appear that the train-or-pay tax levy scheme was most effective. In 1990 the Ministry of Finance determined that only a fifth of the tax credits offered were actually taken. But by 1998, two-thirds of companies subject to the tax levy considered it successful; three quarters of firms that trained reported increased adaptability and commitment on the part of employees. However, it was noted that small- and medium-sized enterprises need help in identifying training needs, and that employees needed incentives to take up training.

In the discussion of the various presentations there seemed to be a clear preference for pursuing multiple strategies in order to ensure that increased investment in learning is forthcoming, and that such investment meets the diverse needs of different groups of individuals and different types of employers. Klaus Luther[34] warned against policies that placed undue emphasis on vocational training at the expense of more general education and training. Others questioned too heavy reliance on approaches such as individual learning accounts insofar as they shift too much the burden of finance onto individuals, serve only persons who are already motivated to undertake learning activity, and thereby have regressive redistributive effects. But obviously there are limits to an excessively open-ended approach to testing different policies. Paul Oomens[35] and others stressed the importance of being able to evaluate the net effect of various measures and the extent to which particular approaches complement others or substitute for other approaches. Even though employers and individuals might be expected to assume most of the burden of financing workplace and adult learning, government needs to play a role in providing the mechanisms and institutional arrangements for facilitating those financing roles.

5.   Priorities and remedies

The chairs of the four working groups gathered in plenary session to report on issues that emerged in their respective sessions, and discuss priorities to guide future actions and policy. A number of key points were identified for each of the sectors considered.

Early childhood education and care

- Early childhood education and care contribute to "social capital" insofar as they help develop productive, responsible and participative citizens.

- There is need for increased public investment in early education and care to ensure equity and quality.

- More effort is needed to measure programmes' outcomes and effectiveness, and ensure accountability.

Compulsory and upper secondary education

- Government is responsible for financing and shaping education at this level, and for ensuring opportunities for early school leavers and poorly qualified adults to have adequate access to learning opportunity at this level; if schools are to play a role in providing such opportunities, they may require extra resources.

- As schools change to improve opportunities for lifelong learning, they should ensure that they prepare young people for more than vocational education and training.

- As lifelong learning becomes more widely practised, training at this level is likely to become more market driven; this will make it important that quality criteria are clear and respected.

- In particular, it is important that shifts in financing mechanisms, such as greater reliance on outcome-based financing, do not exacerbate inequalities by creating incentives for schools to try to cream off the best students.

Post-secondary education

- Individuals from low-income groups are more sensitive to time and cost when it comes to considering post-secondary education; there are strong intergenerational effects when valuing the costs and benefits of education.

- Firms use qualifications in hiring and compensation decisions; it is important that learning and training outcomes are recognised (through mechanisms such as Assessment of Prior Learning), even if such outcomes are not at the degree level.

- The direct and indirect costs of post-secondary education can be important barriers to firms and individuals; mechanisms are needed to reduce such costs; however, in developing such mechanisms, it should be kept in mind that on the one hand, savings instruments do not help families in lower socio-economic groups whose opportunity to save is limited, and on the other hand, low income individuals may be unwilling to incur debt.

Workplace and adult learning

- This should be funded by public authorities, employer, and individuals; financing by individuals could be facilitated through mechanisms such as *individual learning accounts.*

- Workplace training is the responsibility of the firm and/or union. Individual learning accounts should be used to develop skills that may promote future employability; such training should complement workplace training, not substitute for it.

- Individual learning accounts should be designed to finance direct as well as indirect costs; as such they should make it possible for individuals to take account of the cost of time to participate in lifelong learning, whether it is the cost of foregone earnings or leisure.

- It is not enough to address the financial barriers to lifelong learning; social support, guidance and counselling also may be necessary for success.

6. Mapping policy responses

In the concluding plenary session, speakers representing the perspectives of public authorities, employers and individuals, presented their views on how to address the problems that arise in ensuring adequate resources for lifelong learning.

Leif Hansson,[36] speaking on behalf of the OECD Business and Industry Advisory Committee (BIAC), outlined one approach to facilitating the accumulation of substantial capital sums for investment in lifelong learning, by establishing "competence assurance" in which employers and employees share costs of individual participation in lifelong learning. Under the scheme, employers and employees contribute equal amounts into an insurance fund (from 1 to 5% of annual salary); employees can draw against the fund to pay the direct cost of learning activities (fees, books), as well as the indirect cost (in the form of a reimbursement to the company for the cost of the employee's salary paid during training). Companies have the option of paying higher contributions into the fund; for example, Skandia trebles the company contribution on behalf of employees with low levels of qualifications. An insurance model was chosen in order to increase the mobility of the funds when employees change employers, and to provide security for the contributions in case an individual dies, or the company goes out of business. One hundred companies in Sweden have adopted this approach, with 40% of employees participating; so far there has been a good mix between men and women, and between less- and more-qualified workers.

163

Lil Ljunggren Lönnberg outlined a slightly different approach to individual learning accounts that is expected to be implemented in Sweden in 2002; it is an approach for which she provided details during the workshops. While stressing the importance of governments taking account of the full range of barriers to lifelong learning, she underlined the role of individual learning accounts as a mechanism that enhanced *individual choice*, while also providing a basis for co-financing of lifelong learning. Such an approach is needed as learning becomes more widespread amongst adults. The government undertook an initiative five years ago to raise educational levels among adults. Since then 500 000 persons have participated and increased their salaries as a result. Information technology can help minimise the cost of expanding learning opportunities; indeed distance education opportunities have expanded, and teachers are being trained to work more effectively with computers in the classroom. But individuals will need to take responsibility for choosing what training and education to follow, as well as financing some of the cost.

Robert Harris[37] argued on behalf of the OECD Trade Union Advisory Committee (TUAC) that, in view of the fact that earlier economic progress was based on human capital investment, employers cannot afford *not* to invest in lifelong learning; but in so doing it is important to remember the vulnerable groups in society and design programmes that address their lifelong learning needs. He recognised that affordability depended on contextual factors. He noted that lifelong learning cuts across a number of areas, *e.g.* social services, education and unions (both general and teachers' unions), and there is need to deal with all of the stakeholders both in and outside government. The consultative process has to be real, and there is need to address issues at the national level (funding in particular), regional, sectoral (industry) and local (employer) levels. Resources issues cannot be addressed in isolation from the *quality* and *accessibility* of learning activities.

Bernard Legendre[38] noted that though, on average, more than a third of all workers have access to training, accessibility varies for different groups, rising to 53% for engineers, and to 70% for skilled workers. Accessibility can be improved through use of new technology to deliver training, through better information on learning opportunities, and through increased recognition of skills and competences acquired through experience (through mechanisms such as the *bilan des compétences*). In France vocational training typically is publicly funded; however, within the public sector, the national government role is declining, while that of regional government is increasing. He noted that in the transition to a shorter 35-hour work week, the collective bargaining might be extended to treat training differently.

Benjamin Levin[39] questioned whether lifelong learning is about credentials or something broader; after all, in Canada skill requirements change more slowly than skill levels, and many workers complain their current skills are under-utilised. He also warned against excessive reliance on rates of return as a guide to policy; if investment in training with high rates of return is increased, the supply of skilled individuals rises and puts downward pressure on wages. He emphasised the importance of keeping equity objectives in mind, since individuals with high human capital are already participating in training, and less qualified persons have been falling further behind. He also urged that progress on lifelong learning not be traded off against early childhood education and care, since young children in difficulty often are the children of parents who are in difficulty. No matter what measures are adopted, policy design has to be careful since we are working in a new area and so the implications are not totally understood. Resources are an issue. Government will be involved, but to what degree and with what partners, and through what mechanisms; various incentives and support to learners (through tax credits and grants) might be helpful; collective bargaining should be involved. However, officials need to be wary of trying to transfer foreign experience.

In the ensuing discussion, Conference Rapporteur Donald Verry and others raised a number of concerns about direction of policies and strategies bearing on resources for lifelong learning:

- There was broad support for increased public investment in ECEC to set the stage for lifelong learning.
- There seemed to be broad acceptance of the idea that individuals and employers assume some responsibility for financing because of the limit of government to assume more responsibility.
- It was observed that adjustment in working time could be one component of strategies for sharing costs. Increased time for lifelong learning might be achieved by employers and employees agreeing to forego some reduction in production and leisure time, respectively. However, there was question as to whether employers would pass costs on to consumers in the form of higher prices, or employees through lower salaries.
- There was wide agreement that collective bargaining needed to play a strong role in developing mechanisms, particularly those based on co-financing, and to address the division of financial responsibility for learning activity that is closely related to enterprise needs, vs. that which is related to individual needs.
- There was concern that though employers and individuals are likely to contribute more to financing lifelong learning for adults, this should not displace public resources already being allocated for education and training.
- There was considerable concern expressed about the need to redress the very unequal pattern of participation in lifelong learning; it was argued that, notwithstanding the general importance of the principle of co-financing by individuals and employers, governments have responsibility for ensuring the financial means for persons at risk.
- A number of participants expressed scepticism about the capacity of learning accounts and other schemes based on loans and/or savings to increase learning by the least advantaged; it was observed that non-resource factors such as family responsibilities strongly influenced motivation and access, and that these need to be addressed as well.
- However, certain participants who were familiar with experimental approaches such as individual learning accounts noted that such approaches appeared to have positive impacts on the learning activity of persons from groups that typically are under-represented. Such approaches were seen as reducing the financial risk of training decisions taken with a long-term view of returns.
- Various actors do not share the same goals, or the same time horizons; so negotiation is needed as well as a variety of mechanisms, including information, consultation/ negotiation, reliance on tax policy.
- In view of the considerable experimentation with mechanisms such as individual learning accounts, it was argued that evaluations were needed to better inform public authorities and other actors as to what are the strengths and weaknesses of different approaches.
- Though much of the discussion centred on policies and institutional arrangements to facilitate investment in adult learning, there was wide agreement that there are important resource and finance issues in other "sectors" of lifelong learning.

In the concluding working lunch, Julie Bettney[40] and Joxerramon Bengoetxea offered concluding remarks from a more political perspective. Deputy Minister Bengoetxea welcomed

165|

the focus of the conference. He acknowledged the high political profile of lifelong learning as a strategy increasing employability and supporting citizenship; but he noted the lack of attention in past discussions to the question of how lifelong learning would be financed. He argued that it would be wrong to rely entirely on market forces to resolve the financing issues because of risks of social exclusion for the least advantaged. He encouraged public authorities to encourage experimentation and innovation, but that such efforts be evaluated.

Minister Bettney underlined the importance of lifelong learning as part of a strategy to revitalise New Foundland after the collapse of the fishing industry in the early 1990s. Certain themes that ran through the conference, such as choice and joint action by multiple actors, appear in debates at the provincial level. In the current climate in which 70% of provincial spending is on social programmes, Minister Bettney noted that the provincial government places high priority on investment in social and economic development and the shift to a knowledge-based economy. Government is not seen as having all the answers; partnership between community and governments is crucial for achieving the goal.

Notes

1. Panellists include Winfried Heideman, Hans-Böckler-Stiftung, Germany; Judith Maxwell, Canadian Policy Research Networks; Chiel Renique, Confederation of Netherlands Industry and Employers; Joan Wills, Institute for Educational Leadership, Washington, D.C.; Avrim Lazar, Human Resources Development Canada.
2. Naomi Karp, Director, National Institute on Early Childhood Development and Education, US Department of Education.
3. Fraser Mustard, Founders Network, Canadian Institute for Advanced Research.
4. Barbara Martin-Korpi, Deputy Assistant Under-Secretary, Ministry of Education and Science, Sweden.
5. Kirsten Eknes, Assistant Director General, Ministry of Children and Family Affairs, Norway.
6. Marta Morgan, Acting Director General, Social Policy, Strategic Policy, Human Resources Development Canada.
7. Donald Verry, Professor of Economics, University College London, United Kingdom.
8. Abrar Hasan, Head, Education and Training Division, OECD.
9. Frans de Vijlder, Policy Advisor, Ministry of Education, Culture and Science, Netherlands.
10. Sharon Mason-Singer, Deputy Minister, Ministry for Children and Families, British Columbia, Canada.
11. Annelise Hauch, Head of Section, Ministry of Education, Denmark.
12. Charles Ungerleider, Deputy Minister, Ministry of Education, British Columbia, Canada.
13. Torkel Alfthan, Head of Unit, International Labour Organisation (ILO), Switzerland.
14. Patrick Brunier, Regional Coordination, Mouvement des Entreprises de France (MEDEF), Nord Pas-de-Calais, France.
15. Sarah Elson-Rogers, Project Manager, European Centre for the Development of Vocational Training (CEDEFOP), European Union.
16. Eivind Heder, Deputy Director General, Ministry of Education, Research and Church Affairs, Norway.
17. Veronica Lacey, President, The Learning Partnership, Canada.
18. Anders Vind, Education Advisor, Danish Confederation of Trade Unions.
19. John Scott, Senior Policy Analyst, Ministry of Education, New Zealand.
20. Annika Persson, Head of Section, Ministry of Education and Science, Sweden.
21. Elie Cohen, Policy Advisor, Ministère de l'Éducation nationale, France.
22. Hyunsook Yu, Senior Research Fellow, Korean Educational Development Institute, Korea.

167

23. Paul Davenport, President, The University of Western Ontario, Canada.

24. David Stewart, Head of Division, Scottish Executive Enterprise and Lifelong Learning Department, Scotland, United Kingdom.

25. Raymond Ivany, President, Nova Scotia Community College, Canada.

26. Stefan C. Wolter, Executive Director, Swiss Co-ordination Centre for Research in Education, Switzerland.

27. Thomas Townsend, Director General, Human Resources Development Canada.

28. Joxerramon Bengoetxea, Deputy Minister for Labour and Social Security, Basque Autonomous Region, Spain.

29. Angel Calderón, Professor of Economics, Centre for Economic Studies, Mexico.

30. Nicholas Fox, Learning and Development Manager, The Learning and Business Link Company, United Kingdom.

31. Lil Ljunggren Lönnberg, Commissioner, IKS Commission on Learning Accounts; CEO, Municel, Sweden.

32. Kay Cheesman, Head of Education, The Link Group, United Kingdom.

33. François Duranleau, Directeur des Politiques de main-d'œuvre et des relations extérieures, Ministère de la Solidarité sociale, Québec, Canada.

34. Klaus Luther, Director, Reforms in Education and Lifelong Learning, Federal Ministry of Education and Research, Germany.

35. Paul Oomens, Senior Policy Advisor, Directorate for Technology Policy, Ministry of Economic Affairs, Netherlands.

36. Leif Hansson, Senior Vice President, Strategic Business Development, Skandia Life, Sweden (representing BIAC).

37. Robert Harris, President, Education International, Switzerland (representing TUAC).

38. Bernard Legendre, Chef de service pour la Formation Professionnelle, Ministère de l'Emploi et de la Solidarité, France.

39. Benjamin Levin, Deputy Minister, Ministry of Education and Training, Manitoba, Canada.

40. Julie Bettney, Minister for Human Resources and Employment and Minister Responsible for the Status of Women, New Foundland, Canada.

Bibliography

ATKINSON, A.B. (2000),
"The Tall Story of Widening Inequality", *Financial Times*, August 15.

BARNETT, W.S. (1995),
"Long-term Effects of Early Childhood Programs on Cognitive and School Outcomes", *The Future of Children*, Vol. 3, No. 5, pp. 25-50.

BEHRMAN, J. and BIRDSALL, N. (1983),
"The Quality of Schooling: Quantity Alone is Misleading", *American Economic Review*, Vol. 73, No. 5. pp. 928-946.

BERMAN, E., BOUND, J. and MACHIN, S. (1998),
"Implications of Skill-biased Technological Change: International Evidence", *Quarterly Journal of Economics*, November.

BERRUETA-CLEMENT *et al.* (1984),
Changed Lives: The Effects of the Perry Pre-school Program on Youths through Age 19, The High/ Scope Press, Ypsilanti, MI.

BLAIR, M.M. and WALLMAN, S.M.H. (2001),
Unseen Wealth: Report of the Brookings Task Force on Understanding Intangible Sources of Wealth, Brookings Press, Washington, DC.

BLAU, D.M. (2000),
"Child Care Subsidy Programs", NBER *Working Paper* 7806, National Bureau of Economic Research, Cambridge, MA.

BYNNER, J. and EGERTON, M. (2000),
"The Social Benefits of Higher Education: Insights using Longitudinal Data", Centre for Longitudinal Studies, Institute of Education, London.

CAMERON, S. and HECKMAN, J.J. (1998),
"Life Cycle Schooling and Educational Selectivity: Models and Choice", *Journal of Political Economy*, April.

CAMERON, S. and TABER, C. (2000),
Borrowing Constraints and the Returns to Schooling, NBER Working Paper No. 7761.

CAMPBELL, N. (1999),
The Decline of Employment Among Older People in Britain, Centre for Analysis of Social Exclusion, London School of Economics, CASE Paper 19.

CARD, D. and KRUEGER, A.B. (1996),
"School Resources and Student Outcomes: An Overview of the Literature and New Evidence from North and South Carolina", *Journal of Economic Perspectives*. Vol. 10, No. 4, pp. 31-50.

CASPER, L.M. (1995),
"What does it Cost to Mind our Preschooler?", *Current Population Reports*, US Bureau of the Census, Washington, DC.

COLEMAN, J.S. *et al.* (1966),
Equality of Educational Opportunity, US Government Printing Office, Washington, DC.

CURRIE, J. (2001),
"Early Childhood Education Programs", *Journal of Economic Perspectives*, Vol. 15, No. 2, pp. 213-238.

DISNEY, R. and WHITEHOUSE, E. (1996),
"What are Occupational Pension Plan Entitlements Worth in Britain?", *Economica*, Vol. 63 (250), pp. 213-238.

EDWARDS, K. (1997),
"Individual Development Accounts: Creative Savings for Families and Communities", Center for Social Development, Washington University, St. Louis, Missouri.

GLYN, A. (2000),
"Unemployment and Inequality", in T. Jenkinson (ed.), *Reading in Macroeconomics*, Chapter 10, Oxford University Press, Oxford.

GLYN, A. and SALVERDA, W. (2000),
"Employment Inequalities", in M. Gregory, W. Salverda and S. Bazen (eds.), *Labour Market Inequalities: Problems and Policies of Low-wage Employment in International Perspective*, Oxford University Press.

GOTTSCHALK, P. and SMEEDING, T.M. (1997),
"Cross-national Comparisons of Earnings and Income Inequality", *Journal of Economic Literature*, Vol. 35, No. 2.

GREEN, F., ASHTON, D., JAMES, D. and SUNG, J. (1999),
"The Role of the State in Skill Formation: Evidence from the Republic of Korea, Singapore, and Taiwan", *Oxford Review of Economic Policy*, Vol. 15, No. 1, pp. 82-96.

GREENAWAY, D. and HAYNES, M. (2000),
"Funding Universities to Meet National and International Challenges", University of Nottingham, School of Economics Policy Report.

HANUSHEK, E.A. (1986),
"The Economic Effects of Schooling: Production and Efficiency in Public Schools", *Journal of Economic Literature*, Vol. 24, pp. 1141-1177, September.

HANUSHEK, E.A. (1996),
"Measuring Investment in Education", *Journal of Economic Perspectives*, Vol. 10, No. 4, pp. 9-30.

HECKMAN, J.J. (1999),
"Policies to Foster Human Capital", NBER *Working Paper*, No. 7288.

HECKMAN, J.J., LAYNE-FARRAR, A. and TODD, P. (1996),
"Human Capital Pricing Equations with an Application to Estimating the Effects of School Quality on Earnings", *Review of Economics and Statistics*, Vol. 78, No. 6, pp. 562-610.

HECKMAN, J.J., LOCHNER, L., SMITH, J. and TABER, C. (1997),
"The Effects of Government Policy on Human Capital Investment and Wage Inequality", *Chicago Policy Review*, Vol. 1, No. 2.

HECKMAN, J.J., LALONDE, R.J. and SMITH, J.A. (1999),
"The Economics and Econometrics of Active Labor Market Policies", in O. Ashenfelter and D. Card (eds.), *Handbook of Labor Economics*, Vol. 3A, Elsevier, Amsterdam.

HIPPLE, S. (1999),
"Worker Displacement in the mid-1990s", *Monthly Labor Review*, July, pp. 15-32.

HOBCROFT, J. (2000),
The Roles of Schooling and Educational Qualifications in the Emergence of Adult Social Exclusion, Centre for Analysis of Social Exclusion, London School of Economics, CASE Paper 43.

HOXBY, C. (1999),
"Where should Federal Education Initiatives be Directed? K-12 Education vs. Higher Education", in M. Kosters (ed.), *Financing College Tuition: Government Policies, Social Priorities*, AEI Press, Washington, DC.

HOXBY, C. (2000),
"Does Competition among Public Schools Benefit Students and Taxpayers?", *American Economic Review*, Vol. 90, No. 5, pp. 1209-1238.

IKS (Swedish Commission on Individual Learning Accounts) (2000),
Press Release 29/5/2000 and English Summary of Interim Report on *Individual Learning Accounts*, IKS – A *Stimulus for Lifelong Learning*.

JOHNSTONE, D.B. and SHROFF-MHETA, P. (2000),
"Higher Education Finance and Accessibility: An International Comparative Examination of Tuition and Financial Assistance Policies", Center for Comparative and Global Studies in Education, University at Buffalo, SUNY.

KATZ, L. and MURPHY, K.M. (1992),
"Changes in Relative Wages, 1963-1987: Supply and Demand Factors", *Quarterly Journal of Economics*, February, Vol. 107, pp. 35-78.

KRUEGER, A.B. (1999),
"Experimental Estimates of Educational Production Functions", *Quarterly Journal of Economics*, Vol. CXIV, No. 2, May.

KRUEGER, A.B. and WHITMORE, D.M. (2001),
"The Effect of Attending a Small Class in the Early Grades on College Test Taking and Middle School Test Results: Evidence from Project Star", *The Economic Journal*, Vol. 111, No. 468, January.

LALONDE, R.J. (1995),
"The Promise of Public Sector-sponsored Training Programs", *The Journal of Economic Perspectives*, Vol. 9, No. 2., Spring.

LAYARD, R., MAYHEW, K. and OWEN, G. (1994),
Britain's Training Deficit, Avebury, Aldershot, UK/ Brookfield, USA.

LINDBECK, A. and SNOWER, D.J. (2000),
"Multitask Learning and the Reorganisation of Work: From Tayloristic to Holistic Organisation", *Journal of Labour Economics*, Vol. 18, No. 3, pp. 353-376.

LOCKYER, L., PATTERSON, J. and HARPER, B. (1999),
"Measuring Effectiveness of Health Education in a Web-based Learning Environment: A Preliminary Report", *Higher Education Research and Development*, Vol. 18, No. 2. pp. 233-246.

LYNCH, L. (1992),
"Private Sector Training and the Earnings of Young Workers", *American Economic Review*, Vol. 89, pp. 299-312.

LYNCH, L. (1994),
Training and the Private Sector: International Comparisons, Chicago University Press, Chicago.

MALCOLMSON, J., MAW, J. and MCCORMICK, B. (1997),
"General Training by Firms, Contract Enforceability and Public Policy", University of Southampton, discussion paper.

MARTIN, J.P. (2000),
"What Works among Active Labour Market Policies: Evidence from OECD Countries' Experience", OECD *Economic Studies*, No. 30, pp. 79-113.

MISHEL, L., BERNSTEIN, J. and SCHMITT, J. (2001),
The State of Working America, Cornell University Press, Ithaca, New York.

NARDONE, T., VEUM, J. and YATES, J. (1997),
"Measuring Job Security", *Monthly Labor Review*, June, pp. 26-33.

NEUMARK, D., POLSKY, D. and HANSEN, D. (1997),
"Has Job Stability Declined Yet? New Evidence for the 1990s", NBER *Working Paper* 6330.

NICKELL, S.J. (1997),
"Unemployment and Labour Market Rigidities: Europe versus North America", *Journal of Economic Perspectives*, Vol. 11, No. 3, pp. 55-74.

NICKELL, S. (1999),
"A Picture of the Job Insecurity Facing British Men", LSE Centre for Economic Performance, December.

NICKELL, S. and BELL, B. (1995),
"The Collapse in Demand for the Unskilled and Unemployment Across the OECD", *Oxford Review of Economic Policy*, 11(1), pp. 40-62, Spring.

OECD (1996),
Ageing in OECD Countries: A Critical Policy Challenge, Social Policy Studies No. 20.

OECD (1996a),
Lifelong Learning for All, Paris.

OECD (1997),
Education at a Glance, Paris.

OECD (1997a),
Employment Outlook, Paris.

OECD (1998),
Education at a Glance – OECD Indicators, Paris.

OECD (1999),
Education Policy Analysis, Paris.

OECD (1999a),
Employment Outlook, Paris.

OECD (2000),
Education at a Glance – OECD Indicators, Paris.

OECD (2000a),
Finding the Resources for Lifelong Learning: Progress, Problems and Prospects. Synthesis of Country Reports, DEELSA/ED(98)9, Paris.

OECD (2000b),
Employment Outlook, Paris.

OECD (2001),
   Education at a Glance – OECD Indicators, Paris.

OECD (2001a),
   Education Policy Analysis, Paris.

OECD and STATISTICS CANADA (1997),
   Literacy Skills for the Knowledge Society, OECD/Human Resources Development Canada and
   Statistics Canada, Paris and Ottawa.

ONTARIO CHILDREN'S SECRETARIAT (1999),
   Early Years Study: Final Report.

PRAIS, S.J. (1995),
   Productivity, Education and Training: An International Perspective, Cambridge University Press,
   Cambridge.

SCHWEINHART, L.J. (1993),
   Significant Benefits: The High/Scope Perry Preschool Study through Age 27, The High/Scope Press,
   Ypsilanti, MI.

SHERRADEN, M., JOHNSON, L., CLANCY, M., BEVERLY, S., SCHREINER, M., ZHAN, M. and
   CURLEY, J. (2000),
   Savings Patterns in IDA Programs, Center for Social Development, Washington University in
   St. Louis.

STEGMAN, M.A. (1999),
   Savings for the Poor: The Hidden Benefits of Electronic Banking, Brookings Press.

STEVENS, M. (1994),
   "A Theoretical Model of On-the-Job Training with Imperfect Competition", *Oxford
   Economic Papers*, Vol. 46, pp. 537-562.

TEMPLE, J. (1999),
   "The New Growth Evidence", *Journal of Economic Literature*, Vol. 37, No. 1, pp. 112-156.

TOPEL, R.H. (1997),
   "Factor Proportions and Relative Wages: The Supply Side Determinants of Relative
   Wage Inequality", *Journal of Economic Perspectives*, Vol. 11, No. 2, pp. 55-74.

UK GOVERNMENT (2001),
   Savings and Assets for All, The Modernisation to Britain's Tax and Benefit System, No. 8, HM Treasury,
   London.

UK TREASURY (2000),
   Value for Money Drivers in the Private Finance Initiative, A Report by Arthur Andersen and
   Enterprise LSE commissioned by The Treasury Taskforce.

US DEPARTMENT OF LABOR (1999),
   Futurework: Trends and Challenges for Work in the 21st Century, Washington, DC.

US NATIONAL RESEARCH COUNCIL (2001),
   Eager to Learn: Educating Our Preschoolers, National Academy Press, Washington, DC.

VERRY, D. (1998),
   "Some Economic Aspects of Early Childhood Education and Care", University College
   London, Department of Economics, Discussion Paper 98-06.

WALKER, J. (1991),
   "Public Policy and the Supply of Child Care Services", in D. Blau (ed.), *The Economics of
   Child Care*, Russell Sage Foundation, New York.

173

WEIKART, D.P. and SCHWEINHART, L.J. (1991),
"Disadvantaged Children and Curriculum Effects", New *Directions for Child Development*, No. 53, pp. 57-64.

WENGLINSKY, H. (1998),
"Does it Compute? The Relationship between Educational Technology and Student Achievement in Mathematics", ETS *Policy Information Report*, Princeton.

WOLTER, S.C. and WEBER, B.A. (1999),
"Skilling the Unskilled – A Question of Incentives?", *International Journal of Manpower*, Vol. 20 No.3-4, pp. 254-269.

OECD PUBLICATIONS, 2, rue André-Pascal, 75775 PARIS CEDEX 16
PRINTED IN FRANCE
(91 2001 21 1 P) ISBN 92-64-19667-6 – No. 52191 2001